12.00

5

Nueva Granada

NUMBER SIX

Tarleton State University
Southwestern Studies in the Humanities

NUEVA GRANADA

Paul Horgan
and the Southwest

ROBERT FRANKLIN GISH

Texas A&M University Press
College Station

The paper used in this book meets the minimum requirements
of the American National Standard for Permanence
of Paper for Printed Library Materials, Z39.48-1984.
Binding materials have been chosen for durability.

♾

Library of Congress Cataloging-in-Publication Data

Gish, Robert.
    Nueva Granada / by Robert Franklin Gish. — 1st ed.
       p.   cm. — (Tarleton State University southwestern studies in the humanities ;
  no. 6)
    Includes bibliographical references.
    ISBN 0-89096-640-0 (alk. paper)
    1. Horgan, Paul, 1903– —Knowledge—New Mexico. 2. New Mexico—In liter-
ature. I. Title. II. Series.
PS3515.06583Z658 1994
813'.52—dc20   94-29267
                                                          CIP

To George Day and Tom Pilkington

To Jerry Bradley and Jim Harris

To El Suroeste, la Tierra del Alma

Contents

Preface   ix
Acknowledgments   x

Chapter
  Nueva Granada   3
  Albuquerque as Recurrent Frontier in *The Common Heart*   12
  Calliope and Clio: (River Muses)   25
  The Biography of Place   39
  New Mexico's Own Chronicle Revisited   45
  Calculating the Distance   58
  Legacy: The Great Literatus   67
  The Centuries of Santa Fe: A New Perspective   73
  Completive Polarities: Interview   80
  The Enduring Values of Paul Horgan: Interview   111

Notes   121
Bibliography   129
Index   133

Preface

I FIRST HEARD ABOUT PAUL HORGAN when I was a boy growing up in Albuquerque, New Mexico—the *Nueva Granada* of my youth. Each month my eighth-grade English teacher would shepherd a class of rowdy and rambunctious readers into a stubby, faded yellow school bus and we would head for the Ernie Pyle Branch of the Albuquerque Public Library. Ernie Pyle was much the favored son in those years just after World War II. He had brought fame to the Duke City and I always lingered a bit longer than some of my friends at the display of his works in one of the side rooms of the library— once the famous war journalist's home.

Ernie Pyle was not the only famous Albuquerque writer, I soon learned. There were others—of quite uneven and varying accomplishment, though I knew little of literary criticism at the time. Paul Horgan was one of these local writers and much renowned, the librarian informed us during her prideful orientation lectures to the fidgeting horde before her.

Horgan, we were told, wrote about the Southwest, our spot on the map, and a special kinship developed in my imaginings. His histories of New Mexico, especially his stories about Santa Fe and about the Spanish and Indian battles at Acoma, increased this bond. And I remember one rather solitary, worn oak library table where, in late afternoon one early December day, I sat enthralled as I read stories from *Figures in a Landscape*.

Being a Southern Baptist boy, I found Horgan's writings and the Catholic assumptions and ambience of his stories brought me no small enlightenment about the Catholicism that surrounded me, in school and in my larger forays with my family into the small villages, some of which were traceable back to the days of Juan de Oñate and the Spanish conquest of that ageless land they christened *Nueva Granada,* a land so long revered more than claimed by its American Indian inhabitants. *Nueva Granada,* New Mexico, my state, the place where I was born at a time so very recent in and outside of the scheme of time, of history.

Other pursuits soon replaced the pleasures of the reading table at that small landmark library and I drifted away from the pleasurable reading of other books by Paul Horgan or by any other author. Required reading in high school college preparatory classes usually focused on the Trojan War or the life of Napoleon or a report on *Crime and Punishment,* an apt title for my lethargic and truant literary ways at that time.

It was, perhaps, just as well that Paul Horgan and I parted company for a while. For he was to write many more books during those intervening decades of the 1950s, 1960s, and 1970s, and I was to learn much more about my southwestern homeland—and about defining myself in relation to it—through books and in spite of them.

By the 1970s Horgan had himself long since moved East, to his own birthplace, and I had moved to the Midwest. It was there, and largely because of and through my rediscovery of Horgan's vast number of fine and often vast books that I was able to endure the exile which life offered (at least in topographical terms) on a glacier-etched, black-soiled terrain a thousand miles from home. My spirit often swooned in search of the Sandia and Manzano mountains and the lavalands, which always bounded my sense of place and my centering in it.

Not only did I begin reading Horgan's writings again, I began writing about them in turn. And in the process of becoming acquainted with Horgan and his Southwest I came to know my Southwest, our *Nueva Granada,* if you will, in a new albeit literary light. That light shone back, however, on the actual landscapes of the Southwest as I traveled back and forth between Iowa and New Mexico on various holiday trips, journeys which soon took on the proportions of spiritual pilgrimages much more than hedonistic getaways.

Through reading *No Quarter Given, A Distant Trumpet, The Peach Stone, Far From Cibola, Whitewater, Josiah Gregg and His Vision of the Early West, The Thin Mountain Air, The Heroic Triad, Conquistadors in North American History, Mountain Standard Time, Lamy of Santa Fe, Mexico Bay,* and many relatively more obscure instances of Horgan's writings, I gained a new and ardent regard not just for *Nueva Granada* and the lives and landscapes, the diverse races and cultures that people it and Horgan's histories and stories, but for the writing act itself and the transcendence, the joy associated with the talent of a master word portraitist like Horgan.

Horgan is convincing in his insistence that he is not exclusively a southwestern writer, for his many novels and stories with their setting in the American East are compelling, too, in their realization of the spirit and substance of place. He is, to be sure, a writer East and West, an American author, a world-class writer and prose stylist. But for me, reaching all the way back to the first excitements of reading, which came from actually comprehending the words he had put on the pages that first turned in front of my wide eyes in that wondrous little Albuquerque library, Horgan remains one of the premier western American writers.

My own personal rediscovery of *Nueva Granada* through Paul Horgan was an adventure that still excites and sustains me. These selected writings on Paul Horgan are testimony to that adventure—and a salute.

Robert F. Gish
San Luis Obispo, Calif.

Acknowledgments

THE LITERATURE OF THE AMERICAN WEST is grand and vast. It is a literature easiest to know if you live it. And you live it by knowing not just the empty, wild and glorious places signified as "West," but the people of the West and their histories as they interact with geography, geology, ambience, and overall spirit of place.

Two critics who, for me, opened up whole new vistas on the literature, the history, the people, and the places of "West" are George Day and Tom Pilkington. In knowing them, talking with them, and in reading their writings I am ever so much closer to seeing and knowing the significance and magnificence of America's real and imagined Wests. And it is their friendship that helps give it meaning. Jerry Bradley and Jim Harris were among the first editors to publish my earliest writing on Paul Horgan, and they have, through the years, continued to share with me their enthusiasm, especially in their own poetry, for the "common heart" and soul of all Southwesterners. Among editors, Noel Parsons, and Bonnie Lyons too, are due a special thank-you for their continuing encouragement and faith in my western writings as well as my own personal westering. We know the continuities of Texas in New Mexico and New Mexico in Texas. David Farmer and David Weber at Southern Methodist University know too the grand significance of Horgan's and our Southwest. Warren Baker, Robert Koob, and Paul Zingg have my Far-West gratitude. My family has my abiding love. Lasting thanks go to Julian Concepcion.

As for Paul Horgan, he has shaped my own personal vision of

West and my motives as a writer. He is, to my mind, the quintessential writer's writer and remains heroic in his westering word ways, quests, and accomplishments—and in his resolute dedication to his art through his long, professional, and prolific life as a writer.

Acknowledgment should also be made to the following publications and journals where versions of many of these essays or the bibliography first appeared: the *New Mexico Humanities Review, Southwest Review, Prairie Schooner, Southwest American Literature,* the *Hawaii Review,* the *Bloomsbury Review, Texas Books in Review,* the *Chicago Tribune,* and the *Facts on File Bibliography Series.*

Nueva Granada

Nueva Granada

W. SOMERSET MAUGHAM GENERALIZED that authors reach the height of their powers between the ages of thirty-five and forty. Then for the next fifteen or twenty years, Maugham believed, authors produce their best work. But as everyone knows, generalizations generally don't hold—especially with something as individual and inscrutable as literary talent. *Mexico Bay,* Paul Horgan's twelfth novel in a career that has lasted more than half a century, proves a bold and beautiful exception to Maugham's generalization. (Horgan will turn ninety-two on August 4, 1995, and that date will invariably coincide with another fall release, another new book.)

At the age of seventy-nine when he published *Mexico Bay,* Horgan had lost none of the magic, none of his sensitivity to structure and sentence, pattern and rhythm that was present when he won the Harper Prize novel contest for his first novel, *The Fault of Angels,* in 1933; when he achieved one of his most impressive and organic unions of form and content with *Far From Cibola* in 1938; or when, with *The Thin Mountain Air* in 1978, he finished the poignant account of growing up, known as the Richard trilogy.

Paul Horgan remains one of America's most distinguished living writers. Though his literary career now spans more than a half-century and forty books, he continues to sustain a prolific pace of writing and publishing. Born in New York state and reared in Albuquerque, Horgan has used a variety of fictional settings. Interestingly, Texas is one of the places he comes back to again and again in his portraits of *Nueva Granada,* as Horgan, after the Spanish colonizers, initially referred to it.

Mexico Bay shows just how strong the claim of Texas is on the writer. Subtitled "A Novel of the Mid-Century," which for the most part means that the story takes place (like so many of Horgan's novels) during World War II, *Mexico Bay* depends for much of its effect on the contrasting ambience of three locales: upper New York state, Washington D.C., and Texas—both the Gulf area, from Port Isabel to Corpus Christi, and the Panhandle near Amarillo. Canada also figures into the settings of the novel.

At least in part, depending on the reader's geographical biases, *Mexico Bay* can thus be read as being "about" any one or all of those places. Jonathan Yardley, for example, in his review of the book for the *Washington Post,* suggests—not surprisingly, given his readership—that the heart of the story takes place in the nation's capital, wartime Washington, with "the excitement of uniting behind a 'just war.'" As the title implies, however, the plot, characters, themes and overall structure, the interplay between people, place and idea all converge in Texas, in *Nueva Granada* made newer, on the Gulf of Mexico.

Certainly Horgan prefers not to think of himself as a Texas writer—or even a southwestern or regional writer. But Texas has attracted a special portion of his talent since the 1920s and 1930s when he first began to write. It was Lawrence Clark Powell who, in an address entitled "Great Constellations" given before the El Paso Library Association in 1977, referred to Horgan as "the dean of Southwestern writers," part of the grouping of stars which "illuminated West Texas and southeastern New Mexico" and included J. Frank Dobie, Tom Lea, José Cisneros, Carl Hertzog, Maud Durlin Sullivan, and Horgan's lifelong friend, Peter Hurd.

Technically, Horgan's *Nueva Granada* includes New Mexico, California, Arizona, and Texas—at least these are the states which serve as settings for his southwestern fictions and histories. Growing up in Albuquerque and then living and working in Roswell for almost forty years, Horgan naturally was drawn to northern and southeastern New Mexico. The argument can be made that even though

Albuquerque and Santa Fe, and to a much lesser extent Taos, influenced him greatly, they were more than matched by Roswell and the Pecos Valley—in fact, all of southeastern New Mexico, known because of its attitudes and atmosphere as "Little Texas." As such, Little Texas and the Roswell area figure prominently in Horgan's Texas novels and stories. And although the literary establishments of northern New Mexico, particularly the Santa Fe of Witter Bynner, Haniel Long, Oliver La Farge, and others, did much to enhance Horgan's career, that too was matched by the recognition and encouragement given to him by John McGinnis and the Dallas-based *Southwest Review.* As the fiftieth anniversary edition of that illustrious Texas journal reveals, with its lead essay by Horgan ("About the Southwest: A Panorama of *Nueva Granada,*" first written in 1933), Texas editors and readers were some of Horgan's earliest fans.

Horgan published four more essays in the *Southwest Review* into the 1950s, including portions of what would become his first masterwork of history, *Great River* (1954). For that work, of course, even before the Bancroft and Pulitzer prizes, Horgan was given the Carr P. Collins Award by the Texas Institute of Letters. And again in 1971 the Texas Institute of Letters gave him the Jesse H. Jones Award for his finest Texas novel, *Whitewater.* In 1972 Horgan delivered a major address, entitled "Toward a Redefinition of Progress," before the Philosophical Society of Texas; and in 1973, he received the Western Literature Association's Distinguished Achievement Award (which he accepted with another important address, this one on the advantages and disadvantages, the "pleasures and perils," of regionalist writing and aesthetics), at the University of Texas at Austin. Previously, one of Horgan's most revealing statements on regionalism, this time in the context of regional painting, occurred in 1954 on the occasion of the dedication of Peter Hurd's "South Plains Mural" in the rotunda of the museum at Texas Tech University in Lubbock. Most recently, in September, 1991, the DeGolyer Library at Southern Methodist University established a major Horgan archive. My comments on that occasion are included later in this volume.

Certainly *Great River* as a history of the Southwest over four centuries and as a metaphor for the region's characteristic convergence of valley with plains and mountains is rightfully regarded as being as much about Texas history as that of Mexico and New Mexico. Many of Horgan's best works, long and short, derived in one way or another from the years he spent exploring, researching, and traveling up and down the Rio Grande, preparing himself to write *Great River.* For example, one of his very best Texas stories—a novella really—*The Devil in the Desert,* is the story of an old priest who makes his last tour of duty upriver from Brownsville, into the wild brush country to the northwest. There he confronts Satan clothed in the body of a snake, and engages in a final, hallucinatory debate with his old antagonist. The work clearly deserves to stand beside Willa Cather's *Death Comes for the Archbishop* for its similarity of regional and religious themes.

Horgan, then, gets the most out of his materials, including his experiences; although by saying that, I do not mean to suggest that he repeats himself. However, the more than forty books he has produced during his long career definitely form a whole, simultaneously various and new, but consistent in themes, settings, and characters. *The Peach Stone* (1967), a volume incorporating stories from four decades, indicates just how much of a whole Horgan's writing is. In these stories are found much that anticipates the Texas novels, *Whitewater* (1970) and *Mexico Bay.* Those interested in discovering the roots of these two novels should also consult the overlooked libretto, *A Tree on the Plains* (1943), and *A Lamp on the Plains* (1937), the second part of an unfinished trilogy which began with *Main Line West* (1936). The allusions in *Whitewater* to *A Tree on the Plains* are readily apparent. Similar literary embryos are found in *The Peach Stone* in a story such as "So Little Freedom" (first published in 1942), which is indirectly a Texas story; and in another story of youth, much like *Whitewater* and utterly Texas in locale and flavor: "In Summer's Name" (originally published in 1940).

The titular tale of the short story collection, "The Peach Stone" (1942), is itself as much about Texas, certainly about a man who came from Texas and who was Texan to the depth of his being, as it is about Weed, New Mexico—a fictional town in the Little Texas area of southeastern New Mexico and around Roswell. "The Huntsman"

(1949), also included in *The Peach Stone,* is set along the Pecos Valley, along the "carved clay banks of the red Pecos River . . . fertile and prosperous in the wilderness of dry plains all around, graced by the far-distant lift, loom and day-long change of the southernmost Rocky Mountains." This is a story about people very much like those who inhabit Belvedere, Texas, in the novel *Whitewater.*

Mexico Bay is a self-contained work of art, and the reader, to enjoy it, need not first read all of Horgan's Texas writings—be they history, opera, novel, or short story. The lure of Texas for Horgan, nevertheless, is strong in *Mexico Bay,* and its origins can be traced back to his earlier writings.

A little-known example of Horgan's Texas stories is "Rain in Laredo," first published in the *Saturday Evening Post* in July, 1963— almost twenty years before *Mexico Bay.* Assuredly this story about a secret past shared by a father and his son is by no stretch of the imagination as aesthetically successful as *Mexico Bay.* But the narrator and central character in the story does carry with him into his maturity the memory of Texas and what happened one night in Mexico, eight miles across the border near Nuevo Laredo. And in that memory and consciousness of his own history and that of Texas and Mexico during the 1930s, when the government was harassing the Catholic clergy, and the 1840s, the time of the Mexican War, reside a parallel motive and basis for the characterization and hero of *Mexico Bay.*

The similarities between the narrator of "Rain in Laredo" (both in his youthful, remembered self as an eighteen-year-old rebel and in his mature, respectable, fatherly self finally reconciled with the social and family expectations of his name, W. Borden Dryden III) and Howard Debler, a prizewinning historian of the Mexican War, are at first glance not all that clear-cut. Debler, for example, is a native Texan whose feel for the Gulf area, and especially the Rio Grande Valley and the historic areas around Port Isabel, go far in enabling him to understand the Mexican War and to write about it while isolated near Amarillo in his father's home on the high plains. Conversely, W. Borden Dryden III is from Buffalo, New York, and by implication either an attorney or a businessman, knowledgeable in the ways of settling family estates and comfortable in his materialistic successes.

The historian, Howard Debler, in *Mexico Bay* does not overtly relive any historical scenarios such as those in "Rain in Laredo." His adventures related to the Mexican War are more of the mind than are Dryden's; and his descriptions (Horgan's descriptions filtered through Debler's consciousness) of the battles and their settings around the mouth of the Rio Grande, and before that of the Gulf area as it was first noted by the pseudohistorical Nicholas Broughton, fictively the cartographer of Francis Drake during his explorations of "Mexico Bay" in 1567, are lyrical and beautiful. But Debler does have his adventure: he falls in love with and eventually rescues from a drift toward alienation and death the novel's heroine, Diana Wentworth.

While Dryden in "Rain in Laredo" is an artist merely by self-identification and aspiration, Debler is—although a historian and ostensibly a recorder of objective fact—also an imaginative artist. Another artist in the novel, and one whose conduct represents a fuller extension of Dryden's bohemian ways, is the painter, Benjamin Ives. In the course of the story, Ives steals Diana away to the Texas Gulf, away from the respectable, easy life afforded her first in New York by her father, George MacDonald, and then by the flamboyant playwright and wag, John Wentworth. Diana's movement back and forth between the different kinds of artistic but action-oriented men in her life provides the nodality of the story, a convergence that, similar to that in "Rain in Laredo," involves a damaging wind storm and rain.

Readers will come to *Mexico Bay* with various geographical preferences, having perhaps read several of Horgan's earlier works. Obviously, *Mexico Bay* will mean much in itself to Texas readers who can identify with Horgan's uses of Texas history and geography, real and imagined, as a basis for his narrative. But for those readers who sense there is something more behind all of Horgan's implicit fascination with the Gulf of Mexico and with the people who across the years have experienced it and responded to it as explorers or artists, as builders and settlers, there is much to ponder in Horgan's earlier writing. And a case of sorts can be made, although he would probably cringe to hear it, for Horgan as a Texas writer of long duration, long infatuated with the sublime beauties of *Nueva Granada* and "Mexico Bay" as a place and as metaphor. As such, if Horgan is not a native son he is an adopted one.

Another truly significant thing about *Mexico Bay* as one of the latest installments in Horgan's long list of novels is that it highlights not just his own ability as a novelist, but brings to mind as well, in the very fabric of the novel itself—its action and theme—his career as a Pulitzer Prize-winning historian and biographer, and as an amateur painter. In addition to being consistent and prolific, Horgan, over the years, has been versatile. And his claim to being a true American man of letters—all the truer for the scarcity of the breed—may be seen to culminate in *Mexico Bay* wherein Horgan's own experiences with the theatre, with literature, with painting, and with the military life all converge. Horgan has always been one to incorporate in varying degrees his own biography into his art. *Mexico Bay*—in some ways and particularly at this late-life stage the most comprehensively biographical of all his works—offers support for the assertion that Horgan, as man and author infused into the composites that here make up his four main characters, is his own best hero. To say this is not so much a matter of ego as it is art.

As a novelist and historian, Horgan is at once regional and trans-continental. The great American themes of the East's contact with the West, both in terms of the settling of the frontier and of the West's backtrailers to the East, have always preoccupied him. And so it is again in *Mexico Bay*, in all its diverse settings. It is, again, the Gulf of Mexico, especially the areas around Brownsville and Boca Chica at the mouth of the Rio Grande, and the city and bay of Corpus Christi, that provide the convergence of place and motive for the story. For it is there that the lives of the book's characters dramat-ically cross and recross, in terms of the story's present and in terms of the historical past of the Mexican War of 1846–48, and the sixteenth-century explorations of Sir Francis Drake and his navigator, Nicolas Broughton.

Some might read the novel as the fictive biography of Diana MacDonald Wentworth and of her adventures and misadventures with her four men: her father, George MacDonald, a wealthy newspaper publisher who fought with Pershing in his punitive expedition against Pancho Villa in 1916 and who dies on a courier mission off the coast of South America in World War II; John Wentworth, the older man and debonair playwright whom she marries as a surrogate father and then leaves for much the same reason; Benjamin Ives, an Iowa farm boy become a free-spirited painter who, after adopted patronage by Wentworth and coercion into a curiously malicious and tempting *ménage-à-trois*, whisks Diana off to the wildly irresponsible and happy beaches of the Gulf, where, though he leads her to independence, he leaves her with sorrowful memories of his profligacy and violent death; and, lastly, her eventual deliverer and solace, Howard Debler, an academic whose two passions, to write a definitive history of the Mexican War and to marry Diana, are realized only after years of waiting and a climactic series of harrowing events. Read this way, *Mexico Bay* does have a kind of budding feminist relevancy to the story's present of the pre- and postwar 1930s and 1940s.

Surely Diana Wentworth is convincing as woman and as type. But it is really the men in the book who prove most fascinating—on their own terms, again as men and as types, but most especially in their relationships with each other as they vie in turn for Diana's affections. Horgan has dealt fleetingly and sensitively with homosexuality before, most notably in *Whitewater,* and he has seemingly forever been interested in male friendship and companionship so that a litany of his fictive male companions (whether soldiers, artists, or children), usually foils of weak and strong, intellectual and physical, subservient and dominant, could easily be recited. And Horgan has often utilized the lovers' triangle to great effect in his novels. But never has he been quite so provocative, so ambiguous yet explicit, about the physical/spiritual attractions that can exist between two men as he is here in the network of rivalry, jealousy, and voyeurism that he constructs between John Wentworth and Benjamin Ives.

Ultimately, however, in terms of character, this is Howard Debler's book. He seems Horgan's closest counterpart, Horgan's consciousness. His own best hero. It doesn't take much distortion of the boundaries of fiction and biography to see Debler as Horgan, working away, in method and in perception, on the magnum opus of *Great River*—the years of research, the interruption of the war, the field notes, the flourishes of word-pictures when it comes to evoking the sublime moods and magnitude of *Nueva Granada,* of the great southwestern landscape. Debler is victorious, nobly and happily so, in his quest for success in his writing and in his life. As a tall Texan in love with the American West as a place and as idea, as story and history, he has his predecessors in much of Horgan's fiction. For Debler and for Horgan the notion of the Gulf of Mexico, or as Drake's navigator calls it in the epigraph from which the novel takes its title, "Mexico Bay," amounts to inspiration, amounts to a metaphor for the awesome riddles involved in an artist's journey toward art. And readers can be thankful that Paul Horgan is still in passage, W. Somerset Maugham notwithstanding.

Albuquerque as Recurrent Frontier in *The Common Heart*

Before I can say I am, I was.
—*Wallace Stegner,* Angle of Repose

Maybe everyone has a kind of early West within himself, which has to be discovered, and pioneered, and settled. We did it as a country once. I think plenty of people have done it for themselves as individuals.
—*Paul Horgan,* The Common Heart

INSIDE ONE COPY OF HIS 1942 NOVEL, *The Common Heart* (New York, 1942), Paul Horgan wrote, "Frank—our Albuquerque—with best of everything in return of [*sic*] years of work and friendship." It's an apt inscription for a book about the common heart of humanity, Hispanic, Indian, and Anglo, past and present—all set against the changing yet recurrent frontiers of rivers, mesas, mountains, streets, and buildings of that spot in the Southwest, that part of New Mexico known as Albuquerque, Horgan's own "growing up" hometown.

Certainly *The Common Heart* is about more than Albuquerque in an almanac sense of place. It is about process, about discovery, about growth, and regeneration. In a metaphorical sense, and in an ultimately mythic sense, Horgan in *The Common Heart* takes various people (his characters and his readers) through what might be called the "frontier" experience of living—the discovery and rediscovery of self in others, a recurrent process that links the past to the present, person to place.

Through Horgan's deft naturalistic humanism—his linkage of the mental and emotional landscape to the geographical—and his lyrical rememberings and wonderments, the reader shares in much more than a rendering of the shifting frontiers common to love and goodness, truth and beauty, frontiers common to high novelistic art.

As most readers of Horgan know, frontier as process for him is closely linked with journeying West, with turning Southwest for health and regenerative wholeness. This is reflected autobiographically in Horgan's own removal as a boy to Albuquerque because of his father's illness, a condition young Horgan grew up with in his home and in the city itself, a place, a "frontier" sought out by tuberculosis patients because of its sun and climate. From Horgan's early novel *No Quarter Given* (1935) to *The Thin Mountain Air* (1977), New Mexico as medical frontier, a place for healing and regeneration, is constant and recurrent.

The Common Heart is perhaps Horgan's most poignant (and sweeping) tribute, as the "our Albuquerque" inscription suggests, to Albuquerque for all that it meant firsthand to him growing up there, as a "frontier" of youth, and as an emblem of the frontier experience itself, broadly construed, the borderland where the present holds most tentatively various interactions with past, present, and future. Seemingly a nostalgic glance back in time for Horgan in the war years of the early 1940s, the various interactions of history—individual and collective—provide the design of *The Common Heart* and give us its saga effect.

It is certain of these interactions, these key histories, better thought of as interpolated stories of recurrent frontiers in and around Albuquerque, that I want to discuss. Far from being incidental, the interpolated stories of Albuquerque as recurrent frontier contribute significantly to the organic and rhythmic unity of the novel, to the central metaphor of the "common" heart, and to the book's statement that "maybe everyone has a kind of 'early West' within himself, which has to be discovered, and pioneered, and settled" (*CH*, 44).

By and large, Horgan's counterpart, Dr. Peter Rush, is the means for the glimpses of recurrent frontiers encountered in *The Common Heart*. Partly this is due to Dr. Rush's (and seemingly Horgan's) belief that a sense of the past contributes to healing powers, that the spirit needs ministering to as well as the body. Native to the West (the son of a New Mexico rancher and a schoolteacher from Washington, D.C.), Peter Rush, while in medical school in New York, grows homesick and yearns for the Southwest, for New Mexico, its land and its history known to him in childhood: "He sometimes stared out the window over the telephone wires and roofs of 1906 New York, and looked at the pale sky where it was full of light over the invisible river. There to the West was his home. . . . That was where he was born. That was where he belonged" (*CH*, 21).

To feed such an innate attachment for the land of the Southwest and New Mexico, Peter keeps a standing order with a Boston bookseller for original editions of frontier writings by "explorers, travelers, army engineers, who had come to New Mexico long ago" (*CH*, 7). The frontiers of such individuals parallel and are repeated in his own life as a boy growing up in New Mexico and as a man in his return to practice medicine there.

Once married to Susan Larkin (Noonie) and established in Albuquerque as a father of young Donald, and physician to both the wealthy and the poor, he combines his professional calls with explorations of local frontier history, which fills the pages of his western Americana book collection and is accessible in the environs of Albuquerque. Horgan comments on the significance of Dr. Rush's attempts to fuse past and present, history, literature, and life—all underscoring the titular metaphor of the common heart:

> He would go to the country . . . , bringing along his latest book, if it had a trace in it of activity hereabouts in the early days. He would search until he found the very place which the old words described; and then—alive to the past because he felt so keenly in the present—he would see again what had taken place long ago.
>
> What he would see always made him conclude, even in that

landscape made of such dualities as mountains and plain and river, that the one constant thing was man's spirit.

But though he did not know it, it was himself he was seeing in those terms. (*CH*, 7–8)

Such a passage provides us with an early kernel of motive and theme, a suggestion of how things will expand and cohere throughout the novel. Dr. Rush's present and the present of the other characters who are contemporary with him are rhythmically set against this historical recording of earlier days—a recording that is simultaneously (though presented recurrently due to the linear nature of fiction) individual, local, universal and mythic, synchronic and diachronic.

I intend to consider these recurrent frontiers more or less chronologically as they took place in historical time—not as they appear in sequence in the novel, in story time, since Horgan's method is suspensefully to spread out his numerous interpolated tales early and late, recurrently, just as he alternates back and forth from one "present" plot line, one "contemporary" center of consciousness, to another.

One of the earliest Albuquerque frontiers (most fully told in chapter seventeen and entitled "An Old Endurance"), which occupies Peter's attention in several ways, concerns Juan de Oñate's expedition and the colonization of New Mexico in 1598.

During the silver jubilee of the Sister Superior of Albuquerque's Saint Joseph's hospital (which, along with the public library, Borelli's tavern by the Barelas Bridge, Willa Shoemaker's deserted chicken ranch, Summerfield's Drug, the Coal viaduct, the river valley and the sandhills, serves as a major locale in the novel), Dr. Rush discusses the early Spanish generations with the visiting honorary speaker, the Archbishop of Santa Fe. More particularly they discuss a letter in the church records in Santa Fe which points to the birth somewhere close to Albuquerque of the first colonist baby born in New Mexico—born on Christmas Eve to the wife of José Diego de Nájera, captain of the governor's sixteenth-century expeditionary army.

The extension and continuation of brotherly love as embodied in Christianity, in this instance the Catholic faith and the Christmas message, is clearly present here: "The letter went to the Captain-

General de Oñate at the pueblo and capital city of San Juan, telling of the birth, and the quality of omen it had, Christmas Eve, mind you, the anniversary of the birth of Our Lord Jesus Christ, as far as anybody knew, it was the birth of the first child among the new settlers who colonized new Mexico that year" (*CH*, 175). Thus, accompanying the medical frontier is the theological frontier. Settlement means the preservation of health and the continuation of the spirit, of faith.

Dr. Rush had long wondered where the exact spot of this new world birth had been, significant to him as a doctor and as a historian, and he sets about securing a copy of the letter and locating the place. Horgan's version of the letter, appearing in its entirety, is a beautiful testament of faith in God and the community of peoples, where an old faith confronts a new land. Echoing behind the letter, and augmenting the recurrent effect, is Peter's own love for his son Donald, whose birthday and birthday gift of a .22 rifle play a dramatic part in the developing events of the novel (especially chapters ten, thirteen, and twenty—chapters surrounding chapter seventeen and de Nájera's letter).

Moreover, Dr. Rush's relationship with young Bun Summerfield is, in effect, that of a godfather who serves to initiate him into the field of medicine by allowing him to witness an appendectomy as a visiting "Dr. McGinnis" (chapter thirty-eight). And the whole struggle in Peter and Noonie's relationship is to overcome Noonie's self-imposed frigidity and barrenness and allow her to conceive another child—which she does by the novel's end (chapter thirty-nine). Also, the relationship between Wayne Shoemaker and the memory of his dead father reverberates through this conquistador's interpolated tale of fatherly love and settlement. Indeed, all of the love relationships—Peter's and Noonie's and Molly Foster's; Willa's and her husband's memory; Martha's and Bun's—are echoed in this tale, as is the friendship, the brotherhood of Wayne and Donald. Recurrently, expansively, all of these relationships are recorded and embedded in the interpolated story of the letter.

There are enough landmarks mentioned in the letter for Dr. Rush to find what he believes to be the place of a city's beginning—some three centuries later—in the village of Atrisco, on the highway to Santa Fe. He is encouraged by the frontier spirit of endurance evidenced by these early colonists—something he still feels in his own Hispanic patients like Señora Aguirre, to whom he brings medicine on the trip when he discovers de Nájera's sacred shrine. It is a discovery Horgan artfully understates in that what Peter has also found, in effect, is a marker for the growing town of Albuquerque in the 1920s and the metropolis of the 1940s, the portrait of which he also sketches, by projection into the future, elsewhere in the novel.

The past and present fuse in Peter's mind as he lyrically ponders his find by the river and, in the distance, hears a train whistle which tells him: "Things changed. The Spirit endured. Find it, recognize it, respect it, share it" (*CH*, 186). It is a lesson Peter had learned too in the days of his own early West when as a child he dared to die in a desperate swim with two companions across the Rio Grande, a moment that changes his course in life, tempers him for the future, a moment that (in chapter thirty-two) allows him to stare "at the golden-blue sky and what he felt was thanksgiving not that he was alive, but that he had dared to die" (*CH*, 327).

So for Horgan, the frontier experience of life in crisis, life on the edge, teetering on the brink of potential and realization, is a process common to the human heart, the human spirit—a process that is its own reward and that must be recognized, revered, and participated in for health and wholeness of mind, body, and spirit.

In terms of the Peter/Noonie/Molly plot line, the crisis comes in the form of Peter's clandestine affair with novelist Molly Foster, a simultaneous but not totally related suicide attempt by Noonie, his rededication to his wife, her recovery and acceptance of the life force, of spring, a flooding torrent of rain, and a reawakening earth.

A second recurrent Albuquerque frontier, again dealing with Hispanic descendants, involves an interpolated tale told by Peter's friend and sage, the *viejo* Don Hilario Ascarete—"who in his late eighties (Peter believes him to be ninety or older) had reached a kind of tentative survival that could afford to deal only with concerns in life which had connotations of eternity" (*CH*, 123). Don Hilario's tale, although begun as early as chapter eleven, isn't fully told until chapter thirty and is closely interwoven with Peter's visits to Molly Foster's house in Highland Park and a book he loans her by Elias Gray, *The Western Attorney*, published in the 1850s and dealing with the Old Town heroine of Don Hilario's tale, but at a later phase of her career. As Horgan develops this particular interpolated tale, from two converging quarters, Doña Catalina Anonciacion de Gutierrez, belle of Old Town and later Chihuahua City, and Molly Foster, Albuquerque visitor, merge in Peter's mind.

Don Hilario's life is so closely connected with the Old Town part of Albuquerque's frontier as to become a living link with the past of General Stephen Watts Kearny's occupation a full century before Peter's own Albuquerque frontier in the present of the novel. Again, Albuquerque as Old Town (and as Don Hilario) represents the continuance and endurance of the common heart of humanity:

> Nothing delighted Peter more than to see, in the early summer after a violent rainy spring, a little colony of weeds and grass growing out of the tops of adobe walls or earthen roofs. It seemed to him like a compassionate reaching over of the earth's life, to cover as well as support the life of man. It was not a gloomy parable to him, a living grave; it was evidence of the vitality on which all living creatures drew mindlessly, most of the time; but which, he was certain without knowing just how or why, could be explored and used in conscious self-renewal by men if they would only look for their own true nature and find peace within them. (*CH,* 124)

It is just this peace that Peter is looking for, for Molly, for Noonie, for his son Donald; and it is this peace that old Don Hilario has achieved. The old man's name "suited him in a fascinating inner harmony"; and he is portrayed as a "highly humorous man, and a very good man, essentially" (*CH,* 125), who is an all-knowing *abuelo* who can see straight inside his grandchildren and Peter, who also assumes (somewhat reversed in this tale) the role of counseled grandson. Don Hilario, on the frontier of death, is representative of the same spirit of crisis, endurance, and "health" as his own "grandfather," Captain de Najera; the same daring to die that Peter faced as a youth and that Noonie faces. For Don Hilario, significantly, "Going to die was like going to a party, for anybody so old and so full of what might be called death's health: peace and readiness and completion, on earth" (*CH*, 126).

From Don Hilario, out of his aged memory and meditations, Peter hears the story of Doña Catalina, "La Voz," as she was known, and the lives and times associated with the Sanchez place, the house so prominent in Old Town because of its fine old doorway and deep windows—suggestive of entry into past and future frontiers. A celebrated gambler, singer, and lover, Doña Catalina had come to Albuquerque from Mexico and set up a brothel and gambling palace incongruously near the Church of San Felipe de Neri (in the house known as the Sanchez place in the present of the novel), where "she was an exciting addition to the life of the shady river town, a hundred years ago" (*CH*, 283). But before she can establish herself fully as a "great agent for style and goodness in Albuquerque" (*CH*, 287), General Kearny and his soldiers enter the town, heading west across Indian country to California, tactfully yet forcefully securing the province of New Mexico taken for his government. Horgan describes the territorial Anglo military frontier of the Southwest in these words:

> The United States Army marched down the river from Santa Fe under command of General Kearny in 1846. It was a cavalry force, and it had peacefully annexed the whole territory of New Mexico, proclaiming amnesty and bringing a beginning of civil stability to the little towns and pueblos. . . . There had never been such a thing here before, the American General's proclamations were set up and printed right here, and handed around before the ink was dry. Society had more to do than it could manage. There were balls, and suppers, and reviews, drills in the Plaza, and during the few days while the army halted in Albuquerque, the house of Doña Catalina was . . . ringing with bottles and glasses, and the sound of coins on the tables. (*CH*, 287)

As interpolated tale, the ambience of Albuquerque in territorial days is a significant aspect of Don Hilario's story; however, the details of Doña Catalina's thwarted amorous designs on Kearny's Captain Henry Houghton Somers ("He was a well-bred young man of thirty from the little town of Batavia, New York, and had been in the army for twelve years"; *CH*, 288), affords oblique reinforcement of Peter's own extramarital affair with another frontier visitor, Molly Foster, along with reinforcement of the themes of fidelity and perpetuation in love. The captain, more preoccupied with writing letters home to his wife in New York than interested in carousing with Doña Catalina, leaves her gala welcoming party early and precipitates an unknowing insult with resultant hurt feelings. Peter, too, leaves Mrs. Foster out of a sense of renewed love and duty to his wife, Noonie, after her attempted suicide.

Horgan constructs this particular interpolation nicely in that Peter and Mrs. Foster earlier in the novel (chapter thirteen especially) had, ironically, been reading about "La Voz" and her life in Chihuahua City after her rebuff and heartbroken departure from Albuquerque. It was in large part Peter's and Molly's shared reading of Elias Gray's *The Western Attorney* account of Doña Catalina, ten years after the Old Town episode, that had brought them together and served as a focus of their discussions about New Mexico frontier settlement and East-West, European-American, history-story consciousness. Pained, late in the novel, by his goodbye to Molly and her departure, not for Chihuahua City but for California, Peter thinks back to his own more recent past and the parallels involved. "He remembered Molly as she read aloud to him from the description of 'La Voz' by Elias Gray, in *The Western Attorney*. Had there been a prophetic irony in the act? He remembered her voice, its cool, cultivated sound, along with which there always sounded an involuntary catch of breath now and then. He wondered how long such details would have the power to turn his heart over" (*CH*, 295).

And as with the interpolated tale of Diego de Nájera and its association with the medical visit to Señora Aguirre, Peter, after hearing Don Hilario's tale of the days of General Kearny and "high feelings from long ago," literally listens to the old man's heart with his stethoscope, knowing that the more figurative heartbeat heard in a tale out of the historical past was a heartbeat common to all.

Yet another story about frontier Albuquerque in the 1840s, almost the first interpolated tale in the sequence of the novel, involves a War Department report published, like Elias Gray's book, in the 1850s, but dealing this time with the Indian rather than the Hispanic past. Dr. Rush reads with excitement the accounts of First Lieutenant Aubrey Worthing Barton, 6th U.S. Cavalry, concerning an Indian skirmish somewhere east of Albuquerque. True to habit and hobby, Dr. Rush sets out to find the exact location of the battle, the first recorded U.S. Cavalry–Navajo conflict in the area: "Peter knew the town so well, with the images of both a boy's memory and a man's that he knew just the place to go to" (CH, 72). As he drives out on the mesa, past and present Albuquerque begin to merge in Peter's mind. (It should be noted that each of the interpolated tales concerns a different part of Albuquerque, river valley, and mesa and mountain, bringing recurrent union to the dualities of landscape Horgan mentions at novel's opening and quoted earlier here as a kernel passage):

> Albuquerque was clearly indicated on the maps in the old War Department report. Barton told how the land rose sharply some two and a half miles east of the Rio Grande; and that would be roughly just across the railroad tracks today. He told how the sandy course wound down from the much higher mesa. He said they had ridden parallel to the river, but inland, following the base of the sandhills in a generally straight line. They had camped for the night farther to the north, and leaving at dawn, had come six miles by the time the episode took place. (CH, 73)

Approaching the battle site, Peter empathetically recreates the events of the skirmish. As military escort for a civilian surveying party (the kind alluded to in Don Hilario's tale), Lieutenants Barton and McIntyre, his second in command, are attacked and fired upon by a dozen Navajos armed with U.S. government rifles. On the mesa between the mountains and the river, Albuquerque is seen as a "little adobe town . . . among its cottonwoods along the Rio Grande" (*CH*, 77). With textbook precision Barton and McIntyre prove themselves as companions in arms (echoing here the friendship of Donald Rush and Wayne Shoemaker, and of Peter Rush and Jack Winterowd and Ted Barksdale, which play such important parts thematically and in the plot of the novel); they save the civilians, pursue the Navajo into the streets of Old Town, capture them, and turn them over to the Mexican authorities in the plaza.

This episode and Peter's recreation of it serve as something of a bond of friendship and common interest in his first meeting with Molly in that after he leaves the mesa he drives to the nearby Highland Park area of Albuquerque to pay her a professional call as a referred patient from a colleague, Willie Treddinger, in the East. Molly and her dog have also been wandering about in the adjacent sandhills in a state of curiosity about the landscape and its past. And as Peter relates Lieutenant Barton's story to Molly, this common experience with the land and the past brings them together in a friendship that soon develops into love.

Lieutenant Barton's story also provides Peter with the occasion to delve deeper into his own past and the land's—into the past of myth, outside of time. Molly tells Peter that she intuits Albuquerque, the sandhills, as "an almost wholly masculine land"; in effect, an archetypal place:

> I know dozens of places—in the East, the South, the Mississippi country—even California, the West Coast—which don't strike me just that way. They're soft, close, narrow, compromisable lands. Any girl or woman is her own boss if she feels like it, in any town or city, generally. The sun shines, yes, but in such places, it doesn't enter everywhere. The *shadows* out here are burning with light. The country is so great and the jobs that keep us alive on it are so close to the first simplicities that it takes men to do them. It is Adam's own land. Isn't it? (*CH*, 82)

Peter responds with an anecdote from his childhood (related in a sketchy way as early as chapter two when Peter refuses to practice medicine in New York and tells an eminent physician, Dr. Donovan, about his home in the Southwest); he tells of a chance meeting with an old Indian man by the Rio Grande one Saturday morning, allowing Horgan to fuse Molly's observations about Adam's own land with Peter's Albuquerque boyhood and the frontiers of Indian mythology à la Horgan:

> I asked him where he lived, and he made signs and seemed to cover the whole space here, from the river to the mountains, East to West, and he said, "I live in the house of the sun." . . . He was exactly describing where he lived and it had that real spaciousness for him.—And besides, this is what I didn't know then, as a boy: but the sun is the male source of life to the Indians. It is also the holder of fertility. The power of life itself. They use it in ceremonies and paintings and symbols to mean all these things.—I mean, you have arrived at the same answer as the Indians, if you see what I mean. (*CH*, 83)

Unknowingly commenting on Noonie's failure to fit comfortably into Albuquerque living (a struggle also shared by Peter's mother), Molly concludes: "I see exactly what you mean.—It is a man's country, and of course, I think any woman who is a *proper* woman, would be content there, for that very reason" (*CH*, 83). It is a conclusion that arcs back—ahead in the sequence of the book—to José Diego de Nájera and his wife, and their 1598 New Mexico nativity; a conclusion that anticipates Noonie's eventual pregnancy at the novel's expansive close.

In a final interpolation, Peter and Molly actually travel into the timeless frontier of sun mythology on their trip to the cliff dwelling of Hano, not far from Albuquerque. In the deserted dwelling of the Hanos, the "sun children," Peter and Molly are profoundly moved by "an eternal question . . . a question we can answer in the heart, but never in words" (*CH*, 243). Trying to answer the question, the mystery of such a civilization in time and place, Peter and Molly climb to the uppermost level of the dwelling, a ghost city which provides a kind of mythical mirror image of Albuquerque as community. As he looks at the top, easternmost ramp or walkway, Peter speculates: "Good people came there in the first hour of daylight to make their devotions and learn the day. I think they lived here not because they were scared or were bandits, but because this is a noble place for a city, at one with the sky, the plain and the river" (*CH,* 244). And in the most lyrical moment in the novel, just as the two people are most moved by such thoughts, a bird suddenly flies by and cries out: "The sound was like a flash of lightning made hearable. . . . It was like something out of time, that cry and passage, a shearing scream of abstract melody, and it pierced them. It seemed to tell of people gone, and of life surviving (*CH,* 246).

Horgan's *The Common Heart* is like that piercing scream, that passage of such a timeless bird. Like Shelley's skylark, or Keats's nightingale, Horgan has given us varied melodies on a common spiritual motif. Through his interpolations, through his rhythmic juxtaposing of times past with times present as they extend into the future, land and spirit remaining but men and women passing, he has shared with us the pulse not just of recurrent frontiers of an ever-changing yet ever-same Southwest, and a changing but enduring town known as Albuquerque. Rather he has shared the continuing heartbeat of life as an accomplished novelist hears it in his own head and heart and blood, in real and imagined experiences—in an omnidirectional, interpolated world of changing but recurrent frontiers.

Calliope and Clio:
(River Muses)

THE RECEPTION, BY SOME READERS, of Paul Horgan's *Great River: The Rio Grande in North American History* raises some issues in the history and literature of the American West which have a hard time being put to rest. They are essential questions of definition and method at the heart of historiography and literary criticism as they intersect with geography—not to mention other approaches to truth and beauty such as anthropology and aesthetics, the whole matter of social science and art. These are not issues with clearly defined boundaries for they concern such hybrid pursuits as ethnohistory and ethnobiography, fiction and nonfiction, political, economic, and human geography. Which is to say, I suppose, that of the nine legitimate daughters of Zeus and Mnemosyne, Calliope and Clio are only two sisters in a large family. Zeus, of course, with other wives, fathered other children—not all of them female: namely, the Dioscuri, Castor and Pollux.

Jarring as any such image might be, at first thought it would seem more appropriate to ride the waters of the Rio Grande with these twin sons of Zeus and Leda, given the fame of Castor and Pollux for brotherly affection and the protection of sailors. But at second thought, one remembers that the immortal half of that brotherhood, Pollux, spent part of his time with the gods, and the rest of it with his mortal brother, Castor, in Hades.

Signing on for a voyage on the Rio Grande with such lovelies as

Calliope and Clio has to be better than that—even when one realizes that the Great River (as Horgan also found out) though placid, even dry in stretches, has its own hellish dangers, especially when in the company of two sisters who have been known to quarrel about their positions and prerogatives. In the end, however, it is better to sacrifice brawny kinship and naval camaraderie for the ideals of truth and beauty, even if it means going under with the raft.

Published in 1954, the winner of both Bancroft and Pulitzer prizes for history in 1955—the result of a decade of deliberate, dutiful work on that particular project—*Great River* represents a culmination of Paul Horgan's previous histories about the Southwest, beginning with *From the Royal City* in 1936, and including *New Mexico's Own Chronicle* (1937), a historical novel entitled *The Habit of Empire* in 1939, and "About the Southwest: A Panorama of Nueva Granada," a seminal essay published first in the *Southwest Review* as early as 1933.

Representing the beginning of Horgan's second phase as a writer, after his service in World War II, *Great River* anticipates many of his subsequent histories as well, works such as *The Centuries of Santa Fe* (1956), *Conquistadors in North American History* (1963), *The Heroic Triad* (1970), *Lamy of Santa Fe* (1975), another Pulitzer Prize–winner in 1976, and *Josiah Gregg and His Vision of the Early West* (1979), a reworking of an early long essay done by way of introduction to Maurice Garland Fulton's edition of Gregg's diary and correspondence published in 1941.

In addition to these histories, by the age of seventy-nine, Horgan had written fifteen novels, including a historical novel entitled *A Distant Trumpet* (1960) about the Apache-Cavalry wars, and *Mexico Bay* (1982), a novel with a professor of history as one of the leading characters and the hero of the book. Moreover, Horgan has published a good half-dozen volumes of shorter fiction, not including many more miscellaneous short stories in popular magazines and in literary journals.

He has also written numerous biographical appreciations, as he prefers to call them, and countless essays and prefaces, many about the historian's task and about library science. Some measure of his productivity is that over sixty years, since he began writing in the 1930s, Horgan has published fifty-odd books. More than prolific, he has been versatile: historian, biographer, novelist, essayist, poet, dramatist, and he's still going strong.

Because he bends and reshapes the ordinary boundaries of these forms, because he switches from one form to another and redefines genres, he has occasioned some criticism from purists, for the most part academics, who choose to see fiction as one thing and history as another; to view narrative approaches to the recording of history as somehow suspect; in a word, to see story as inferior to history.

Herein resides the controversy surrounding *Great River.* Is it history or is it literature, is it good or bad history, good or bad literature? Can a novelist and a popular one at that, someone who has not been professionally trained as a historian and is therefore considered an amateur historian, write adequate and accurate history? Does Calliope or Clio sit by Horgan's side? An accompanying issue involves Horgan's alleged ethnocentric biases as an Anglo-American historian and a Catholic in favor of what might generally be regarded as elitist rather than populist attitudes concerning the primacy of European civilization and its values, particularly in relation to nature, and geography, over the world views of American Indians, Spanish Americans, Mexican Americans, Chicanos, and Mexicans along the Rio Grande? That is, does Horgan side too obviously first with the aims and attitudes of the Spanish conquistadors and then with the Anglo-American, Yankee stages of colonization?

Either/or propositions are of course notoriously inaccurate and unfair. Sweeping generalizations are generally wrong. *Great River* is a masterwork of both history and literature—albeit flawed. It is a special kind of history as affected by a literary artist, and when approached on its own terms and in light of some of its popularized predecessors, the greatness of its achievement is recognizable. Horgan's intent is clear. In a prefatory letter to his friend, Charles Arthur Henderson, Horgan identifies his kind of history, his own historiography. He seeks first "to produce a sense of historical experience, rather than a bare record"; to do this he tries "to see events, societies, movements, through human characters in action," and "without . . .

departing from the inflexible limits of respectful scholarship [he takes] every opportunity to stage a scene."[1]

In deciding to interrupt the straight narratives of events to describe various ways and customs of the people, Horgan says he takes Herodotus as his model and observes, "Only when events are rooted in the soil of the culture might they seem to have true reality" (*Great River*, vii). Macaulay likewise influenced Horgan's method in that he attempted more to stimulate the reader than to provide an original piece of research. Eugene Delacroix and Allan Nevins are also credited as influences in that Horgan believes "the writing of history, in addition to being a technical craft, is also an art" (*Great River*, vii). Horgan chooses to use modern place names "in order to give the reader an immediate sense of locality" and he opts not to use footnotes or "running references" only because, he says, he does not want to divert the reader's attention from the story. This decision is unanimously condemned by professional, academic historians who criticize *Great River* as history. Although there is at times substance to such bibliographical quarreling, it all too often sounds like the crankiness of pedants. Horgan does include a listing of his sources at the end of each volume, listed by chapters, and does append a complete bibliography. It is clear from his introductory letter that Horgan expected some criticism from historians. Little did he know the extent of the *ire* and rancor *Great River* would occasion.

As mentioned, some perspective on the nature of Horgan's achievement is gained from viewing it in the context of his own life and career as an author and in the context of other histories of the Rio Grande written by colleagues and contemporaries. *Great River* was not Horgan's first or last attempt at representing the history of the Southwest, particularly the Rio Grande Valley. It bears emphasizing that a good portion of all of his writings is focused on the Southwest, on New Mexico and Texas. (Admittedly, Horgan is a transcontinental author and writes about both the East and the West; however, his concern is with the ways in which East and West affect each other through immigration, settlement, and backtrailing.) Although Horgan was born in New York state (of Irish-German ancestry), he grew up in New Mexico, returned to the East intermittently, and then in the 1960s moved to Connecticut where he still lives. This sense of place, of living in the West, is important since for some people, and Wallace Stegner is one, to be a true western writer, historian or novelist, one must be born in the West, born a "square" as Stegner says, and grow up there.[2]

Few would deny that Horgan is a western writer in the general and not stereotyped sense of the word; that is, he lived much of his life in the West and writes about that place as he experienced and imagined it. However, Horgan is unlike any other western writer. He is not to be confused with Ray Hogan or Max Brand or Louis L'Amour of paperback fame. He is a very refined and cultured man of letters, more at home at the opera, particularly the Santa Fe Opera which he helped found, than in an arroyo.

Next, it should be observed that Horgan's *Great River* is not unique, not one of a kind. It is a monumental book to be sure. But it belongs to a larger context of "river books" all to some degree historical/literary narratives, and not all of them American, or if American, not all of them about the Rio Grande—though there are several of those that bear mentioning. Hemingway's comment that all of American literature began with *Huckleberry Finn* must be viewed as more quip than axiom. As Jonathan Raban so eloquently demonstrates in his robust best-seller, *Old Glory: An American Voyage* (1981), Mark Twain did embody an archetype with his version of boy life on the Mississippi. And as significant and as symbolic as the Mississippi River is to an understanding of East-West, North-South vectors of American political and social history, there are many other books about the Mississippi and, indeed, about other American rivers; the Hudson, James, Ohio, Potomac, Missouri, Colorado, Arkansas, Platte, Pecos, Brazos, Gila—and the Rio Grande—each famous in its own way. Thoreau's *A Week on the Concord and Merrimack Rivers* (1849) is recognized as a classic, as is a work like John Graves's *Goodbye to a River* (1961). Horgan was keenly aware of rivers in literature and history if for no other reason than that *Great River* began as a volume in Holt, Rinehart and Winston's Rivers in America series—but it soon spilled over into two volumes and outgrew the length requirements of that series. Horgan's bitterest critic, Frank D. Reeve, criticized him for, of all things, writing the history of a river.

The books closest to Horgan's *Great River* as prototypic historical narratives, however, are those by his contemporaries, Harvey and Erna Fergusson, and by Laura Gilpin—and beyond those authors are similar works like *The Land of Poco Tiempo* (1893), by Charles F. Lummis and much further back the epic of Spanish colonization, *La Historia de Nuevo Mexico* by Gaspar Perez de Villagrá in 1610.[3] Horgan draws extensively from Villagrá's accounts of the 1599 Battle of Acoma in his own early historical novel about that conflict, *The Habit of Empire* (1939). Indeed, if one wants to talk about the beginnings of literature in North America, as Mabel Major and Matthew Pearce say, "Villagrá's poetic chronicle must be accorded place as the first poem about America by anyone who had visited the territory and could give firsthand observation of what he saw."[4]

Since Horgan was librarian at New Mexico Military Institute for many years prior to World War II and was for a short time after the war assistant to the president at NMMI, and was a close friend of the Fergusson family, his *Great River* owes a larger debt than one might first expect to these predecessors. Comparisons of *Great River* to Harvey Fergusson's *Rio Grande* (1931) and to Laura Gilpin's *Rio Grande* (1949) are particularly revealing. And a consideration of Tony Hillerman's *Rio Grande* (1975) demonstrates even more clearly how each author's perception of the river as place, history, and idea varies with each voyage on it. But one essential never varies: southwestern history and literature are both to a considerable extent functions of a spirit of place—of geography and the mind's perception of it, real and imagined.

As for the reader reception of *Great River*, the belief that Horgan is an amateur, inaccurate, and generally inept historian, by implication hardly worthy of a Pulitzer, Bancroft, or any other kind of prize awarded on historiographical merits, centers around two reviews which in tandem quite sarcastically attack the author and his work. (At least one graduate thesis, Catherine C. Mundell's "Paul Horgan and the Indians: *Great River as a Historical Failure*," unpublished University of Texas at El Paso M.A. thesis, 1971, also disputes Horgan's claim to the title of historian.) Though many people do not believe the two particular published attacks are worth a response, it is essential for present purposes to follow their respective and companion points of argument.

Stanley Walker, in the *New Yorker* (ordinarily a friendly magazine which published some of Horgan's earliest writings, then under the pen name of Vincent O'Shaughnessy), took Horgan to task for something as comprehensive as his style, a style Walker calls "New Mexico baroque," a style which he personally doesn't like, a way of writing that he sees as going much beyond Horgan and being an indictment of New Mexico writers generally. Clearly again, eastern sensibilities are not those of the West—or some certain parts of "West" publishing in the East, for Walker also wrote much in Texas. Perhaps Walker resurrects some old Texas–New Mexico rivalries for *New Yorker* readers. Perhaps they couldn't care less. In any event, attempting to be funny, Walker breezily criticizes Horgan's writing, affected too much he thinks by place, by geography. About Horgan's style Walker says,

> Some people will like it; others, with considerable evidence on their side, are bound to be confused and even embarrassed by its occasional lofty pretentiousness. One either thinks New Mexico baroque is great or one doesn't. An odd thing happens to writers who live in the high country, especially in the mystical stretches along the Rio Grande above El Paso. It happened to poor old D. H. Lawrence, to Mabel Dodge Luhan, and to many others—to a lesser degree to such a sound citizen as Miss Erna Fergusson. They see the mountains, the sand, the stars, the cactus, the wrinkled Indians, and they begin to babble about "time" and "space."
>
> At its best, and in moderate doses, this can be fetching literature; at its worst it can be baffling—like something by Dylan Thomas out of Sitting Bull. Mr. Horgan is by no means the most tortured of the victims of this New Mexican disease, but the virus is there.[5]

It is apparent that Walker's satirical glibness about Horgan's response to geography misses much of the complexity of the interrelationship among good writers and among place, history, and imagination. Artists are especially keen to ambience whether they are historians or novelists. Certainly D. H. Lawrence (notwithstanding Horgan's disregard for him too), needs no patronizing adjectives before his name. In his personal account of the Rio Grande's effect on him, Lawrence speaks lucidly enough when he says, "I think New Mexico was the greatest experience from the outside world that I ever had. It certainly changed me forever. . . . The moment I saw the brilliant, proud morning shine high over the deserts of Santa Fe, something stood still in my soul."[6] Horgan too was supremely affected by the New Mexico landscape and by the Rio Grande Valley, which in history becomes a metaphor for the many confluences of culture, event, and personality known as *Great River*—for the Southwest. Horgan's beautiful watercolor field notes testify to this.

When one really listens to what southwestern writers have to say about the importance of place to their writings, Walker's snobbish satire pales into sophomoric silliness. One of the most perceptive (and I mean this in several ways) explanations of how New Mexico and its landscapes influence a writer is that of Chicano novelist—a chronicler and historian in his way too—Rudolfo Anaya. For Anaya, it is landscape—or what many Chicanos think of more endearingly as *la tierra*—which functions as both metaphor and epiphany and allows a writer, in response to geography through imagination and memory, to generate the power and energy, the momentum required to write. This, in part, is what Anaya says about landscape and writing:

> On one pole of the metaphor stands man, on the other is the raw, majestic and awe-inspiring landscape of the southwest; the epiphany is the natural response to that landscape, a coming together of these two forces. And because I feel a close kinship with my environment I feel constantly in touch with that epiphany which opens me up to receive the power in my landscape. I don't believe a person can be born and raised in the southwest and not be affected by the land. The landscape changes the man and the man becomes his landscape. My ear-

liest memories were molded by the forces in my landscape: sun, wind, rain, the *llano*, the river. And all of these forces were working to create the people that walked across my plane of vision. And my vision was limited until I was taught to see the stark beauty which surrounded me. I was fortunate to meet a few, old *ancianos* who taught me to respond to my landscape and acquire the harmony which is inherent between a man and his place.[7]

Questions of ethnohistory and ethnoaesthetics temporarily aside, what Anaya affirms and calls "magic realism" of place is what Stanley Walker derides as "New Mexico baroque." It is a topic long at issue in regional studies, especially in the literature and history of the West which somehow must always reconcile words with sublime geography—and by this I mean landscape plus climate and cultural atmosphere. Thus, the style and substance of a book like *Great River* are, I suppose, inherently controversial to an extent.

Colorado poet Thomas Hornsby Ferril coined the term "landscape mysticism" in attempting to describe how he felt geography affects western writing. The West involves a geography so large that seemingly only larger-than-life characters can cope with it. To Ferril, such assumptions cause writing about the West generally to distort the truth.[8]

In an especially informative study on "The Interrelationships of Literature, History, and Geography in Western Writing," Richard West Sellers comments: "In the Westward movement history paralleled geography. Where America grew greatest in size, the geography was correspondingly more vast and powerful . . . [and] in the open western country the distances and the size of the landforms revealed another relationship to time and space, that is to say man's being brief and infinitesimally small."[9]

In *After the Fact: The Art of Historical Detection,* James West Davidson and Mark Hamilton Lytle demonstrate in their own eminently readable style just how important geography was in Frederick Jackson Turner's theorizing about the nature and location of the western frontier and its recurrent settlement.[10] (That Horgan was influenced by Turner's theory of recurrent frontiers is obvious throughout *Great River*—a point that few if any critics of the work have bothered to evaluate.) Others in the wake of Turner's wave theory have attempted to accommodate history and geography and literature—choosing rightly enough to see them as reciprocal and complementary. Stuart B. James in "Western American Space and the Human Imagination" (1970); Roderick Nash in *Wilderness and the American Mind* (1967); Paul Shepard in *Man in the Landscape* (1967); Henry Nash Smith in *Virgin Land* (1950); Frederick Turner III in *Beyond Geography* (1980); and D. W. Meining in *Southwest: Three People in Geographical Change* (1971)—all of these authors, and others less scholarly but fine, like Marc Simmons and David Lavender, demonstrate just how complex the sisterhood of Calliope and Clio really is. The depth of this complexity is of course traceable back to the first notions of sublimity and landscape in the writings of such authors as Edmund Burke, Joseph Addison, Horace Walpole, and Thomas Gray. But that's another country.

This is mentioned in an attempt to show that behind Stanley Walker's satirical assessment of *Great River* is a body of thoughtful study on the very complicated network of interactions among geography, history, and literature; to show that it is worth investigating how region affects perceptions of both historians and literary artists; to say that inspiration evoked by spirit of place does not *ipso facto* deny "truth," but can enhance it. Style is thus not necessarily merely a condiment, although Walker doesn't seem to suggest this when he poses this final acerbic question about *Great River:* "Pretty [he says], but is it history?" It's a cute but insidious kind of question for it implies that the two terms are mutually exclusive—that by implication history is empirical, quantifiable data, facts, and not art; it suggests even that artistic narrative techniques such as those used by novelists to "stage a scene" are off limits.

According to Davidson and Lytle, when history is reduced to pure social science, history at the expense of story, historians wind up talking only to themselves.[11] Barbara Tuchman, a historian who talks eloquently to the common reader, contends that "the thought applied by the historian to his subject matter can be no less creative than the imagination applied by the novelist to his."[12] Tuchman pointedly asks, "When it comes to writing as an art, is Gibbon necessarily less an artist in words than . . . Dickens? Or Winston Churchill less so than William Faulkner?"[13] She cites Cambridge professor George Trevelyan as the great champion of history as literature addressed to the general reader—not exclusively to the academy. Tuchman confesses that when she writes history she feels like an artist, a person she defines as one having "an extra vision and an inner vision plus the ability to express."[14] University of Virginia professor of English David Levin says flat out to other academics: "We have not talked seriously enough about the art of history."[15] Levin, too, believes that literature is not ornamental to history; good writing is not an afterthought. Levin says, "I hope we have passed the time of which Carl Becker complained when he declared that modern professionals would have considered Francis Parkman a good historian if only Parkman had not written so well."[16]

Princeton sociologist Morroe Berger takes the balanced view that "the separate spheres of science and literature must . . . be appreciated without trying to impose a spurious unity or to stir up a contest."[17] More metaphorically and comprehensively, Wallace Stegner observes:

> Calliope and Clio are not identical twins, but they are sisters. History, a fable agreed on, is not a science but a branch of literature, an artifact made by artificers and sometimes by artists. Like fiction, it has only persons, places, and events to work with, and like fiction it may present them either in summary or in dramatic scene. . . . Objective and sociological novels come very close to history, the difference being principally that history reports the actual, fiction the typical.[18]

The late Frank D. Reeve, a historian known for his work on the Southwest and particularly the Navajo in New Mexico, picked up on Walker's panning of *Great River* and in a twenty-eight-page essay disguised as "A Letter to Clio" in the *New Mexico Historical Review*, responded to Stanley Walker's either/or question by saying yes, *Great*

River "is sometimes pretty, but it is not good history."[19] An expert on southwestern history, Reeve does make some substantive criticisms of Horgan's method and product. But much of what he says reads like trifles. More significantly, the form his criticisms take—that is, a letter to the muse of history (by mocking Horgan's introductory letter to his friend, Charles Arthur Henderson), pointing out to her just where Horgan presumably slipped, where he makes this mis-statement or that, where his methodology is mistaken or his style displeasing—comes across almost embarrassingly like self-aggran-dizement and impertinence. Reeve regrettably overstates his case. "A Letter to Clio" is a classic case of seemingly resentful pedantry by an academic historian stung by the recognition, the prizes, afforded to a historian outside Ph.D. programs and departments of history.

Reeve contends that Horgan was influenced too much by Herodo-tus, the storyteller. Thucydides the critical-minded historian, [Reeve says in his letter to Clio], should have been heeded also.[20] Siding with the scientific camp of the either/or context between Calliope and Clio which he seeks to stir up, Reeve sees a "systematic error" in Horgan's history residing "in building the story along the Rio Grande."[21] In an argument which remains unconvincing, Reeve says,

> A river is not a valid basis for writing history. An author, using such a basis, is forced to become a Procrustes who short-ened or lengthened travelers to fit the size of his beds. The river historian likewise shapes material to fit the preconceived form. . . .
>
> History is the never ending search for the closest approx-imation to the truth of what happened and when it happened. It is governed by accepted canons of scholarship. Many are the workers in the search. The end result is a product of collective effort. He who spreads abroad unsound history, renders a dis-service in the joint effort to find the truth.
>
> Embellishing with a fine literary style enhances the pleasure of the reader, but the *substance*, not the *style*, is the prime consideration. When the historian-artist neglects the former, he renders justice to neither.[22]

In Reeve's reading of *Great River*, Horgan falls short of "accuracy of facts and soundness of interpretation"; it is a failing which in large measure Reeve attributes to an inadequate bibliography, the use of general rather than specific studies, and the neglect of scrupulous, pinpointed footnotes. In addition, Reeve sees *Great River* as too fragmented, disunified, lacking in overall theme with no final summation—merely "a collection of miniatures."[23] To say that Horgan is wrong in structuring his history on the river and then to insist that the book has no central theme is assuredly a contradiction. And insofar as Horgan traces the coming of people to the river over three centuries or more, tells of Indian, Spanish, Mexican, and Anglo-American cultures as they replaced and merged with each other, and stops his story, admittedly somewhat abruptly, with the intrigues of the Zimmerman telegram and Germany's designs on the United States–Mexico borderlands—this in itself does not add up to a lack of unity. The Rio Grande as river and history is continuous. And Horgan's final chapter is appropriately expansive and visionary— linking the ancient valley of the Pueblo Indians with the present and futuristic terrors of Los Alamos, Trinity Site, and the nuclear age.

More legitimate is Reeve's criticism of Horgan's treatment of Indian history. Reeve accuses Horgan of at least implicitly siding with the Spanish and Anglo colonists as superior to the Indians. Others, including historians of the West of the stature of Oliver LaFarge, and Horgan's close friend, Erna Fergusson, also take him to task for seeing Spanish and Anglo cultures as advancements of the individual over the assumed faceless collectivity and conformity of American Indians.[24]

To be sure, in the 1980s the very conception and directionality of the Southwest is more and more obviously an ethnocentric idea. The Mexican-American concept of Aztlán, just like the Spanish quest for Cibola, is to be found in the north—somewhere on the Rio Bravo del Norte, as the Rio Grande was once called—and not in the Southwest. Horgan's views about the Rio Grande and its history, like Frederick Jackson Turner's, are ethnocentric, no doubt about it. If he were to write a history of the Rio Grande today, he might be more sensitive to his Turnerian assumptions of the 1940s. He indi-

cated in an interview with me in 1979 that if, for example, his novel
about Oñate's conquest of Acoma, *The Habit of Empire*, were to be
reissued today, he would stand by his interpretation of historical fact
of savagery on both sides, but add a qualifying preface for the
present-day reader. Each historian is a product of a culture and a
time, conditioned by them, a notion that Carl Becker himself attempted to establish in saying that "every man is his own historian,"
that history is relative to "the personal equation."[25] Had Horgan
been someone else, from a different time, of a different world view,
Great River would be a different book. The mortal historian is by
nature incapable of telling all, surveying all records, relating both
history and story from all perspectives. Even so there is a majestic
presumption involved in invoking the muses of both literature and
history, Calliope and Clio. Exclusive historiography that denies the
nodality of history, literature, and geography will fall far short of
adequately portraying something as encompassing and awesome as
the Rio Grande and the American Southwest. More and more,
syncretic scholars of the American West—Richard W. Etulain and
Don D. Walker, to name two—are demonstrating how impressive a
combined, interdependent method really is.[26] But it is a writer like
Paul Horgan, heroic in his quiet way as the historian-novelist, who
as an imperfect exemplar, takes us to history, stages it in such a way
that we are not merely traveling the pages of a great book; we are also
on the great river, there with Calliope and Clio on the water, under
the sky and sun, on the Rio Grande.

The Biography of Place

WHEN PAUL HORGAN ACCEPTED the Western Literature Association's 1973 Distinguished Achievement Award in Austin, Texas, he spoke eloquently and decisively about "The Pleasures and Perils of Regionalism."[1] The major peril he noted was the common one of definition of terms, particularly when identifying regions of the West, all separate and distinct in geography and in society. Not only does the term "West" shift regionally, Horgan pointed out; it also shifts stylistically—from unconsciousness to stylized self-consciousness. And when this happens, says Horgan, the validity of regionalism disappears: "Where once the term stood for uncommonized local ways, it now stands for any almost comic cartoon-like view of the varied life styles to be found in the physical variations of our land" ("P&P," 168–69).

What Horgan is talking about is essentially the same thing that Wallace Stegner said again when lamenting certain kinds of New Mexico writing, around Santa Fe and Taos particularly, which "wears too much turquoise and pads around too self-consciously in squaw boots."[2] It is this peril that finds compensation in the pleasure of dealing instead with the "actual history and biography of social ways of the West before our time" ("P&P," 170). In "biography" the "primarily human" transcends the "spicily" western, suggests Horgan, and not surprisingly he draws on Cather to make his point:

> Willa Cather . . . left us a wonderful response to human life which merely happened to be circumstanced by a certain locality. It was her beautiful achievement to keep "place" in its

proper place, while reflecting its values and powers in her crea-
tures as they came alive under general vision and empathy for
life at large. In her work—no doubt regarded in Nebraska as
"regional"—it is her lively artistry which holds us for its own
sake—how things are said, rather more than what they are
about. ("P&P," 170)

In her keeping of place in its proper place, Horgan would clearly not
regard Cather's narrative portraits of individuals like Jean Marie
Latour, Joseph Vaillant, or Eusabio as narrative of place; nor would
Horgan think of his life story of Jean Baptiste Lamy, in a limited
sense, to be regional—a "biography" of place.[3] Ostensibly, Cather
and Horgan are writing biographies of persons. The tendency is
understandably to avoid associations of regionalism and place with
mere local color or provincialism. Nevertheless "artistry" and "how
things are said," technique and style, are so very closely functions of
place as to become content, to become what things are about. And at
least for some readers, Santa Fe and New Mexico (not to mention
France, the Middle West, Mexico, Rome, and so on) as place and,
more important, as culture, are so saliently present in Horgan's and
Cather's books that they veritably cross over the commonly distin-
guishable boundaries of setting to become character—the character,
and thus biography, of place.

If character is action it is also place. And the atmosphere and
ambience in *Lamy of Santa Fe* and *Death Comes for the Archbishop*
weights the turning of every page. As Horgan suggests, such a reading
is probably determined by the place of readership. New Mexicans,
naturally, like books about New Mexico. Texans like books about
Texas. But most likely southwesterners, similar to others, like books
that capture essences about *life* in that particular place, books about
the spirit of that place. And that is what both Cather and Horgan
went to such great lengths to experience for themselves—as persons
and as writers—the spirit of persons in place and place in persons.

Perhaps even more obvious instances of this than *Lamy of Santa
Fe* are Horgan's *Great River: The Rio Grande in North American
History* (1954), *The Heroic Triad: Backgrounds of Our Three South-*

western Cultures (1970), *The Centuries of Santa Fe* (1956), and the much earlier collection of stories, *Figures in a Landscape* (1940), wherein Horgan says about persons' relationships with land, in this case the Southwest:

> The great constancy of that land is what the human spirit feels most deeply there. Because the earth's grandeur and power are so frontal in the consciousness of everyone—in contrast to the concerns of men and women who live in closely settled places where the human network is much more active and appears to be ever so much more the real conditioner of lives—it is this landscape which unifies spirit and invites its discovery, to whatever degree a man may be able.[4]

The story of Horgan's coming to write *Lamy of Santa Fe* is itself an example of the effect of place on an artist over a great number of years and is inextricably mixed with New Mexico and Willa Cather. In a detailed series of autobiographical comments, Horgan sets forth the history of his preoccupation with Lamy and relates it to the biographer's art. Horgan had the advantage of hearing about Miss Cather from her youngest sister, Elsie, who was Horgan's freshman English teacher at Albuquerque High School.[5] As a relatively new arrival in Albuquerque, much the frontier town compared to his home in Buffalo, Horgan first found in Cather's early stories—aside from her artistry—a theme which he understood firsthand: the exile and resettlement of physical invalids and of more refined sensibilities facing up against the Philistines.

About his encounter with Cather's early works, albeit retrospectively as he assesses it years later, Horgan in "Preface to an Unwritten Book," says, "Willa Cather used the pathos, the tragedy, of the higher culture, in the person of a great artist, against the uncomprehending society of the frontier West and its Philistine mentality."[6] And precisely against such a theme as this, Horgan and his biographical analogue and, indeed, Cather's and hers—Archbishops Lamy and Latour—seem reflections of what might be considered the biographical myth, or life script, behind Lamy, Cather, and Horgan.

Horgan sees the theme of exile as worked out in Cather's stories as parallel to her "own sense of deracination after the removal of her family from Virginia, with its old traditions, to a raw Nebraska in her girlhood."[7] Nebraska is not the Southwest, not New Mexico or Texas or Arizona or Colorado, to be sure; but the broad outlines of exile out West, in a new world—a fascinating, forsaken frontier—are recognizable in the biographies of both authors and their subject. Horgan has said, "I have derived most of my education informally from the cultural expressions best exemplified in the intellectual and artistic life of the East and of Europe,"[8] and in such a statement the profile of the persona behind *Lamy of Santa Fe* assumes sharper distinction.

After hearing about Cather from her sister in Albuquerque, he actually met her in Santa Fe—the place where they both began their acquaintance with Lamy's legend. Horgan's account of his inadvertent encounter with a working Willa Cather in the La Fonda hotel in 1926 is of interest:

> In the deepest corner of the porch were two steamer chairs, and upon them reclined two ladies whose concentration I disturbed. They were busy with papers and pencils. I have an impression of many accessories—notebooks, opened volumes, steamer rugs against the vagrant breezes which feel cool to someone out of the sun in Santa Fe, perhaps a thermos jar containing hot bouillon, possibly a fly whisk, and what else? If I invent it, it is because I have forgotten, and if I have forgotten it is because the nearer of the two ladies turned upon me a light blue regard of such annoyance and distaste at my intrusion that I was gone too quickly to take more than a sweeping impression of where I had been. But I was there long enough to recognize that it was Miss Willa Cather whom I had interrupted at work with her secretary, and I was already so devoted to her work that my chagrin rose equal to my respect. . . . What was she working on that morning? I did not know, and I cannot now say, but a year later her novel about Juan Bautista Lamy was published.[9]

Horgan further describes this meeting almost in terms of reverence, for Lamy and Cather, and in terms of destiny. In the Santa Fe of youth and early manhood he came to know Lamy and his own need to write about him, as he tells in the same essay: "I came to feel his quality and his effect, and ever afterward, when I went to the cathedral at Santa Fe, or walked along the long wall of the Bishop's Garden, or heard the angelus clapping its rings of sound over the city, he was somewhere behind my thought, my eye, my ear; and one day he would move me to vest him, however poorly, in my word."[10]

Certainly this feeling of Horgan's for Lamy's quality and effect is transferred to the finished biography, itself an act of love, and indeed religion—of Horgan's belief that "however quietly I may state or imply it, my humble relation to creativity is an expression of my religious belief."[11] And Horgan went to devoted lengths to discover Lamy and the various places in his life, places which became a part of his being. In the thirties Horgan visited the room where Lamy had died, "on a narrow bed in the corner . . . in pain, and at peace, on a snowy morning of 1888"; then a trip to Auvergne, the region in France where Lamy was born near Clermont-Ferrand at Lempdes, a village strongly reminiscent of Santa Fe to Horgan; and throughout these and other travels looking for Lamy, Horgan made watercolor paintings—as he says, "a process by which for years I have fixed for myself my impressions of scene and spirit of place for later reference in historical writing." Like Lamy, Horgan journeyed from Santa Fe to Durango, duplicating as closely as possible, although by auto-mobile, the archbishop's trip to Mexico in 1851.[12]

Moreover, in an attempt to know how it felt to become a bishop, in 1957 Horgan arranged to be a close observer, almost a participant, in the consecration of the Most Reverend John M. Fearns—making wash and watercolor drawings during the splendor of a three-hour ceremony repeated through the centuries. As a result, the description of the 1850 raising to the purple of Lamy at Cincinnati's St. Peter's Cathedral is a masterfully sustained and detailed six-page culmina-tion to book two and to the ending of Lamy's Middle West years and his setting forth to Santa Fe (the starting point of Cather's first book in *Death Comes for the Archbishop,* "The Vicar Apostolic"). Here is a description of process as place.

Horgan's combining of painting with his quest for place, and indeed his verbal paintings of *Lamy of Santa Fe,* meet with striking parallels in Willa Cather's famous letter to the editor of *Commonweal,* about how she happened to write *Death Comes for the Archbishop.*[13]

Of all the stories heard and felt during her visits in the Southwest, the story of the Catholic Church interested her most. In the old mission churches "the utterly unconventional frescoes, the countless fanciful figures of the saints, . . . seemed a direct expression of some very real and lively human feeling."[14] In the midst of such an interest in the effect of the Church on human feelings, Lamy became (through the stories she heard) an invisible friend, just as he did to Horgan.

Every time Willa Cather passed the life-size bronze of Lamy before the cathedral in Santa Fe, Lamy's distinguished, "well-bred" looks captivated her. Her interest in Lamy's life crystallized when she read Father William Joseph Howlett's biography of Reverend Machebeuf and the letters translated therein (a source fondly relied upon by Horgan as well).

Cather attempts what she calls "something in the style of a legend," a series of prose frescoes in which character soon yields to something larger: "In the Golden Legend the martyrdoms of the saints are no more dwelt upon than are the trivial incidents of their lives; it is as though all human experiences, measured against one supreme spiritual experience, were of about the same importance."[15] That spiritual experience, Horgan says, is held "in the land, . . . the ultimate entity."

Horgan's essay "In Search of the Archbishop" is his equivalent to Cather's letter to the *Commonweal.* He acknowledges the letter just as he does Father Howlett's book and the "gentle intuitions" that secured Lamy in fiction. This is not to say that Horgan's biography of Archbishop Lamy owes everything to Cather. Rather, it is to suggest that Willa Cather and Paul Horgan share not just a common subject, but experiences, sensibilities, themes, and techniques that are grounded in something that might be termed the "biography of place."

New Mexico's Own Chronicle Revisited

A HALF-CENTURY AFTER ITS PUBLICATION in 1937, Paul Horgan and Maurice Garland Fulton's *New Mexico's Own Chronicle* merits revisiting. The circumstances surrounding its collaborative composition provide a revealing glimpse into southwestern literary history and into the development of Horgan's literary world view. Few readers today know about this unique text—or remember it. It is long out of print. And most existing copies are generally inaccessible, filed away in institutional or personal archives and special collections of one kind or another.

The individuals who do remember or know about *New Mexico's Own Chronicle* are more than likely amateur or professional historians interested in southwestern history or, more particularly, New Mexico history, who think of the book as a paradoxically "handy" anthology, once located, or the repository of some even more difficult to locate primary "histories."

The regrettable aspect of this centers around what might be regarded as the virtual disappearance of a text intended as a popular history for the common reader, a "textbook" of New Mexico history to be utilized, primarily, in the public schools of the state. The road to rediscovery of *New Mexico's Own Chronicle* by readers in search of a "popular" history of New Mexico and the Southwest must probably now begin with readers interested in exploring the intriguing interrelationships manifested in this text between "history" and "literature," historiography and literary history.

New Mexico's Own Chronicle is especially worth reconsidering in the light of current debate among professional historians about the definition of, the effect and value of, narrative history at a time when history, as process and as recording of that process, is most generally regarded as a science rather than an art. Furthermore, *Chronicle*—as a compendium of travel narrative, memoir, personal essay, imaginative and factual tellings—is something of a classic instance of history as autobiography and biography. And, in a related vein, the composition of the book itself offers an interesting case study of a collaboration of its editors as friends, colleagues, and writers who have themselves entered into the chronicle of southwestern literary history.

In an even smaller tangential context, the book represents a beat, an interlude in the "history" of New Mexico Military Institute (NMMI) and the town of Roswell where Horgan lived for so many years, a place that inspired much of his fiction.

Paul Horgan's career and accomplishments as a writer-historian, novelist, and all-around man of letters have eclipsed the career of Maurice Garland Fulton. Horgan has won two Pulitzer prizes as a historian, and garnered many awards and considerable recognition of his fiction—short stories and novels—as an American author as well as a favorite son of the Southwest. Even Fulton, however, occupies a notable spot, locally in Roswell as well as more regionally in southwestern literary history. William E. Gibbs and Alfred L. Castle admirably document Fulton's role as a regional and local historian in their 1980 essay on Fulton in the *New Mexico Historical Review*.[1]

New Mexico's Own Chronicle, then, chronicles much more than a southwestern state and survives as a chapter in the continuing chronicle of New Mexico's larger history. This essay hopes merely to open that chapter and turn a few of its pages. The "chronicle" of how Horgan and Fulton came to write *New Mexico's Own Chronicle*—the history of its conception—is interesting in itself besides having bearing, as one might expect, on the style and substance of the book.

Horgan recalls that "the concept of the book was all Fulton's."[2] Fulton was an English professor at New Mexico Military Institute in the mid-1930s and Horgan was librarian. Moreover, when Horgan was a cadet at NMMI Fulton had been his English instructor and Fulton, as Horgan's senior and to an extent his mentor, had written and edited other works—textbooks on such subjects as Shakespeare and rhetoric, in addition to works of local history, most notably subjects such as Billy the Kid, Lincoln and Chaves counties, and Roswell.

T. M. Pearce, another friend of Fulton's and then editor of the *New Mexico Quarterly,* observed that Fulton was highly esteemed as a New Mexico author in 1936 when Pearce commented in the "Los Paisanos" column of the quarterly that roving book salesmen who stopped by the English office at the University of New Mexico had the utmost respect for Fulton's popularity and reputation as a Southwestern author: "According to Macmillan's salesman, one of the most prolific writers in the country is Major Maurice Fulton, of the New Mexico Military Institute. His reputation is so well established that all he has to do, it seems is to inform this publishing house that he has finished another book, and the contract is sent by return mail."[3]

There is perhaps some sarcasm here in Pearce's recognition of Fulton. Fulton's correspondence confirms that he and Pearce did not always see eye to eye on literary and editorial matters. Nor did they agree on definitions of history and folklore. Fulton, for example, lamented to Horgan in 1950, as a kind of "coda" to a letter about the possible reprinting of *Chronicle,* that he and Pearce were at the moment in a wrangle "over a contribution of the forthcoming issue of his [Pearce's] *Folklore Record.* He does not want what I would like to write and he almost demands that I do what he directs. I claim that what he wants is not classifiable as folk lore, but being derived from documents is history."[4] It seems Fulton was dedicated to his views, ever ready to wrangle.

In spite of Fulton's felicitous association with the Macmillan publishing company, it was Horgan, he attests, who engineered a reprint of Josiah Gregg's *Commerce on the Prairies* with Banks Upshaw company in Dallas and it was with that publisher that Fulton negotiated the publication of *Chronicle.* When Fulton asked Horgan to collaborate with him on the project, Horgan soon agreed. As Horgan remembers the working arrangement, "I had been his student in English class some years earlier and at first felt diffident working *with* him; but it worked out. He was a steady, slow, scholarly worker.

I was rather more ebullient. But we became a working team" (Horgan, 2/18/87). Horgan does not recall which of the historical excerpts he helped choose, or which precise passages of introduction he wrote. He does recall editing the concluding chapter, including his own essay taken from the *Southwest Review,* on New Mexico's future; an excerpt on Albuquerque from Harvey Fergusson's *Rio Grande;* and another essay, on Santa Fe, by playwright, author, and Harvard graduate removed to the West, Philip Stevenson. And Horgan likewise wrote all the caption material for the illustrations: "Probably we discussed every final selection, etc. MGF was sometimes remote and testy, many times otherwise kindly and permissive of much-junior notions." Gibbs and Castle call the organization of *Chronicle* "characteristic of Fulton's editorial approach and one that he would later use in working with the papers of Josiah Gregg."[5] Certainly Horgan influenced that organization.

What Horgan refers to as "the general shape of the contents," that is, the piecing together of original sources with editorial commentary in a chronological and "chronicle" pattern of, as the subtitle states it, "Three Races in the Writings of Four-Hundred Years," was both unique and derivative. Horgan's close friends and Fulton's acquaintances, Erna and Harvey Fergusson had used such a panoramic approach to New Mexico to varying degrees in *Dancing Gods* (1931) and *Rio Grande* (1931) respectively. Horgan himself had utilized it in his seminal essay, "About the Southwest: A Panorama of Nueva Granada," which ran in the *Southwest Review* in 1933 and was excerpted by Horgan again for *Chronicle* in 1937. Erna Fergusson made more of the notion of New Mexico's chronicle or panorama when, in her history of New Mexico (1951), she portrayed the state as "A Pageant of Three Peoples." Certainly the "history" of New Mexico itself, its events and lives, invite such a triadic conceptualization— seemingly prototypic or ready made by events themselves. (Monroe Billington, among others, in his study of the African American population of New Mexico, points out that to view the Southwest as merely a "triad" of cultures is to overlook the diverse ethnic and racial mix of the larger West.) Horgan, nevertheless, was so deeply imprinted by the notion of laminated cultures and of Frederick Jackson Turner's explantion of settlement as "recurrent frontiers," that both Horgan's *Southwest Review* essay and *Chronicle* served him well as a source of invention and arrangement in most of his subsequent histories of the Southwest, including *Habit of Empire* (1939), *Great River* (1954), *The Centuries of Santa Fe* (1956), *Conquistadors in North American History* (1963), *The Heroic Triad* (1970), and, to an extent, *Lamy of Santa Fe* (1975).[6]

The personal aspect of Horgan and Fulton's relationship as teacher-student, colleagues at NMMI, and as coeditors of *Chronicle* and collaborators in the two-volume edition of *The Diary and Letters of Josiah Gregg* (Norman: University of Oklahoma Press, 1944) is not without its somewhat darker side of strained relations—mostly, or so it appears, enmity against Horgan and probably envy on Fulton's part. For they neither began nor ended the best of friends. In 1971, long after Fulton's death in 1955, Horgan offered his friend and fellow librarian, Lawrence Clark Powell, a long, humorous caricature but a sadly sensitive and ultimately rather poignant account of his association with Fulton.

Horgan's abilities as a portraitist have served him well in his roles as novelist, historian, biographer, and painter. Whether serious or in parody, he knows how to render a person or personality into essentials. His talents as a satirist are well-known and his book of clerihews amply demonstrates his visual and verbal skills at caricature. His portrait of Fulton is somewhere between the high seriousness of the rendering in *Henriette Wyeth* (1980), for example, and the elegant humor of *The Clerihews of Paul Horgan* (1985).

Horgan was a student in Fulton's English class in 1922, the first year of junior college for Horgan. In Horgan's rendering, Fulton's pedantic mannerisms and behavior caused him much cruel ridicule by cadets at NMMI. Because of his ill-fitting uniforms he soon took the nickname of "baggy pants" or simply "baggy." (A glance at the NMMI annual, the *Bronco,* confirms that cadets have their public, published—semiofficial and expected—nicknames as well.) Fulton's background as a southerner and his insistence on decorum, his habit of speaking with a complaining if cultivated tone of voice, and his overall attempts at instilling discipline by swatting his sprawling and uncomprehending students with his clipboard soon led, or so Horgan speculates, to the killing of one of Fulton's pet cats. (Gibbs and Castle mention that Fulton's office in the basement of Wilson Hall at NMMI was "shared with a motley crew of cats who ate from open cans of sardines and tuna."[7] It was at that time that Horgan, ever fascinated by Fulton's classes, most sympathized with him. Horgan left NMMI in 1923 for study at the Eastman School of Music in Rochester, New York.

When he returned to Roswell in 1926 it was as librarian for his old school. Horgan was then a faculty officer, a captain, and Fulton was a major, eventually to be a lieutenant colonel. In 1933 Horgan won the Harper Prize for his first novel, *The Fault of Angels*. By the time he came to his collaborations with Fulton he was gaining a reputation as a novelist. *No Quarter Given* appeared in 1935; *Main Line West* and *The Return of the Weed*, in 1936—along with, that same year, the small series of narrative histories in *From the Royal City*. And the following year, 1937, *New Mexico's Own Chronicle* appeared more or less simultaneously with *A Lamp on the Plains*. In addition to *Chronicle* Horgan wrote the long introduction to Fulton's two-volume edition of Gregg's diary and letters. In 1979 Horgan published a revised version of this introduction as *Josiah Gregg and His Vision of the Early West* (New York: Farrar Straus Giroux).

While Horgan worked daily, building his skills as a novelist and historian and his reputation as an author in the vanguard of the then burgeoning Southwest "renaissance," Fulton was busy writing as well. Horgan's rather ambivalent yet ultimately disparaging description of Fulton at that time runs like this:

Like the conventional scholar, he lived and breathed in dust—the dust of books undisturbed except by himself; but there was nothing dusty about his mind, which was as orderly as his surroundings were disorderly. He was our distinguished faculty man for some time, as he published his Shakespeare textbook, his books on composition, his edition of Pat Garrett's *Death of Billy the Kid*. Some of us found it privately hilarious that this Mississippi cross between a Dickensian antiquary and a southern gentleman and burlesque officer should become a devotee and an authority on New Mexico's worst badman. He worked for years on a life of Billy the Kid, and the story went that he kept calling it back from Macmillan, his publishers, for new revisions. At his death it remained unpublished.[8]

After classes and school duties Fulton opened up, for whatever public wanted to see the documents and artifacts gathered there, the building now the Roswell Museum, built in the 1930s under the Works Progress Administration (WPA) program. At least this is Horgan's recollection. Gibbs and Castle establish the time of Fulton's assuming the job of curator of the Lincoln County Museum at the age of seventy one, after his retirement from NMMI in 1948. In what Horgan describes as his "aging loneliness and—yes—eccentricity," Fulton also allowed as many as twenty of his cats to inhabit the place. Reportedly, the stench became unbearable and when generous benefactors contributed to the expansion of the museum, Horgan was elected president of its board of directors. He then had the delicate duty of solving the cat population problem. Fulton resisted for a time but eventually relented. Their friendship did not wholly survive the controversy in that Fulton assumed a "swift, fierce, and unremitting hostility" to Horgan. Even so, Horgan offers this tribute: "He always remained for me the teacher who—in his unique way—received my student writing with such sympathy and encouragement, while requiring discipline in my work, that I have been able to make lifelong use of much that I learned from him."[9]

Horgan characteristically took great pride in book design and typography in the production of *Chronicle*. Banks Upshaw and the editor with whom Horgan worked, a Mr. Goolsby, allotted very little money to the production of the book, so Horgan designed the format and jacket. The jacket, Horgan recalls, had to be hand colored to spare color reproduction and "the materials of the physical book were shockingly cheap."[10] Even so, by today's standards *Chronicle* is a sturdy, austere but beautiful book. It runs to nearly four hundred pages and has the feel and weight of the reporting of the four hundred years it chronicles.

It was advertised, fittingly, as the result of the cooperation of a "mature, widely read scholar steeped in the literature and atmosphere of the region"—on the one hand—and "an accomplished and versatile young novelist" on the other.[11] The age and youth of the authors decidedly paralleled the past-to-present span of the subject. That subject was identified on the book's jacket as "a collection of letters, diaries, memoirs, formal historical writings, and documents of state which reflect the daily lives of the inhabitants of New Mexico in various periods of her history."

In a sense, the jacket text promised almost too much—as perhaps did the conception and scope of the book: "This book is a one volume account of the evolution of New Mexico as it is today. It is also an anthology of representative literature pertaining to the entire Southwest. There are selections from rare volumes such as Gregg's *Commerce of the Prairies*, Kindall's *Texas Santa Fe Expedition*. Several of the selections are materials hitherto unpublished in books, taken from manuscripts, newspapers, magazines, and like sources." The type of history attempted in *Chronicle* was promoted in jacket blurbs as informal—emphasizing "social aspects and characteristic details of every-day life that are not often found in histories of the more formal type." The editors, the advertising attested, took all possible pains to make the book entertaining reading. Indeed, the promotion went so far as to claim that *Chronicle* "has all the movement and unity of a novel." Its claim was, in short, as popular, narrative, regional history.

The president of Banks Upshaw was reported as appearing before the New Mexico state board of education to urge adoption of *Chronicle* in history classes throughout the state. The State Department of Education and the state archives and records office have no record of such an adoption ever coming to pass. Horgan and Fulton realized only a pittance in royalties, which would not have been the case if school text adoption had been approved. In 1950, when queries were made by the University of New Mexico Press about possible reprinting, Fulton wrote to Horgan saying, "I doubt very much that the book ever had plates; and I think it was printed from type and the type was destroyed. Didn't we have a contract? I don't remember

. . ."[12] (Fulton, March 29, 1950). Horgan renewed the copyright as late as 1960 but the heirs to Fulton's literary estate remained unknown, at least to Horgan.[13]

Despite the fact that *Chronicle* was not a great publishing success and brought no monetary fortune to its editors, it was well received by reviewers, especially in the Southwest, as might be expected. Moreover, the national press also gave it generous recognition.

In most of the interviews and publicity notices quoted in announcements and reviews, Horgan described the book as amounting to New Mexico writing her own autobiography.[14] The *Fort Worth Morning Star–Telegram* raved about the entertaining and exciting dramatization of the "prehistoric civilizations," the Indian peoples during Spanish occupation, the first years of American occupancy, the effects of the Civil War, the lawless country bandits such as Billy the Kid, the coming of the railroads and the high pitch of mining fever, the entrance of New Mexico into the Union as the forty-seventh state, the rise of old Santa Fe as a new city where artists and legislators look toward the future—all confirming that the contributions of New Mexico's three "amalgamated races to our national culture and folklore is not inconsiderable; the beauty of their land speaks through them in all their works."[15]

The *El Paso Times* described the book as a "contribution both to the regional literature of the Southwest and to the art of historical anthology making," saying in addition that few books about New Mexico had attempted to offer the whole historical process of "this geographically fecund and interesting region."[16] Major Fulton and Captain Horgan were viewed as having tastefully chosen an extract here and an extract there and arranged them into "a fascinating historical mosaic."[17] The *Houston Chronicle* agreed, saying, "[Fulton and Horgan] have bridged the gaps between the different documents quoted with narrations of their own, tying the stories together and making a coherent volume."[18]

Reviewers from the *Tulsa World, Birmingham News, Milwaukee Journal, San Diego Union,* and numerous other dailies all found New Mexico a romantic and picturesque state more than worthy of such an approach. The *Washington Star* referred to the book as a "history of America's current land of the lotus."[19] The *Cincinnati Enquirer* went so far as to say that such a book was more than welcome since New Mexico has "the most glamorous and picturesque history of any state in the union.[20] The *New York Times* concluded that "from the first Indian legend of the beginning of life, to Paul Horgan's concluding essay on the future of New Mexico, . . . [*New Mexico's Own Chronicle*] is absorbingly readable."[21]

Such reception reveals how widespread the mystique of New Mexico was in the public mind and imagination in the 1930s and how naturally receptive popular readership was to a first-hand, autobiographical approach to the land of enchantment "telling" its own story. Horgan and Fulton knew well enough that their attempts at stitching together the diverse narratives of four centuries left much to be desired and fell short of capturing the full force of the processes associated with the name, "New Mexico."

Neither Fulton or Horgan, ironically, even as military men, as "soldier" educators, knew how drastically New Mexico's history was to veer with the developments of World War II, Los Alamos, Trinity Site, and the atomic bomb. Had *Chronicle* pointed to or even hinted more prophetically at such a development and the ironies involved, then the state's mystique would have been all the more awesome in its modern contradiction, convolutions, and resolutions of nuclear science in such an ancient land.

In retrospect, both men realized how relatively innocent and thus quaint their chronicling the developing New Mexico really was. In 1950 Fulton was either euphemistic and evasive—or perhaps deliberately naive or ingenuous—when he reconsidered the role of the atom in the state's story. He knew the book was dated in ways he could not really have imagined. But he was still interested in redoing such issues as games and pioneer life—impressively insignificant when compared to the import, for example, of the Manhatten Project. He wrote to Horgan:

> I have always felt that if the book were to be revived, it should be overhauled rather violently. The discovery of potash and the development of other phases of modernness should be

brought out. I believe an interesting division might be sports and games, both Spanish and Anglo, and Indian. More emphasis should be [given] home life in New Mexico pioneer times. The edition should have a bent more in the direction of the objectives that are put before the young people of today under the name of *social studies*.[22]

Horgan was able to include something of the history of the atomic bomb and the military-industrial influences on New Mexico in the concluding chapters of *Great River* some years later. And nearly thirty years beyond that, in 1981, Horgan had even more definite modifications in mind for any possible reissue of *Chronicle:*

> I have mulled over the desirability, and the possibility, of adding a brief section to the present end of the book, bringing closer down to us in time of a couple of major interpretations of New Mexico's scene so the book will have relevance to new readers who will want a later or updated chronicle. I have in mind Erna Fergusson's remarkable account of the development of Los Alamos and the atomic bomb there, and perhaps an account by Oppenheimer of the first explosion at Alamogordo, whose world implications can be left to the general knowledge of any reader nowadays. Further, I thought of a few pages giving the flavor of *modern* Santa Fe, and have an idea for that excerpt.[23]

Horgan's ideas for extending the "chronicle" underscore the point everyone now fully realizes, especially contemporary southwestern novelists and historians: that the story and history of New Mexico must somehow describe and attempt to explain—or perhaps reconcile—all that Los Alamos, Frijoles Canyon, the Puye cliff dwellings, the Pajarito Plateau, nearby Santa Clara Pueblo, and more distantly, Stallion Gate and Trinity Site, mean in the chronicle not just of New Mexico but of Earth and of human and ecological survival.

To say that as historians Fulton was more the editor/social scientist and Horgan more the artist/storyteller seems accurate enough—

but oversimplified. In a 1983 study of Horgan, I asserted that he is a true humanist and polymath; that Horgan, like his historian characters in such novels as *The Common Heart* (1942) and *Mexico Bay* (1982), is indeed more artist than scientist.[24] Furthermore, I argue that Horgan in his "artistic" history, perceives the Southwest from a decidedly ethnocentric, albeit tolerant and accommodating, point of view. In the tradition of Turner, Horgan writes from elitist rather than populist assumptions about "progress" and "civilization"—assumptions which implicitly view each phase of New Mexico settlement (Spanish and Mexicans dominating Native Americans, Anglos dominating Spanish and Mexicans) as exemplifying Anglo-European humanistic values.

Partly in response to these contentions, Howard Lamar, while conceding that Horgan is indeed a Turnerian, insists that Horgan owes much to the tradition of Francis Parkman, as well, in that *The Oregon Trail* "is one of the first instances of this historian recording and overland trail saga" and that "Parkman's fame . . . rests on his accomplishments as the first American to describe, in a heroic and panoramic way, the rise and fall of imperial France in North America."[25] Lamar sees the similarities between Parkman and Horgan continuing in that just as Parkman saw Europe coming to America via two great rivers and from more directions than just east to west, Horgan too "effects three entrances to the Southwest": north from Mexico in the instances of Coronado, Oñate, and de Vargas; up the Rio Grande Valley from the Caribbean, as by Alonso Alvarez de Piñeda, Narváez, and Cabeza de Vaca, and others; and from west to east, as attempted by Coronado.[26] Lamar sees Horgan as going beyond the limitations of Turner to the omnidirectional history of Parkman, and thus as much interested in all the European entradas as in "American exceptionalism."[27] True as such a pairing of Horgan with Parkman may be, it deserves mentioning too that Parkman's other great legacy, of course, is as a narrative historian, and that in Parkman's narratives, European values are again seen as rightfully reigning over America's indigenous peoples.

Horgan's Turnerian or Parkmanesque Anglo-European values notwithstanding, *Chronicle* reveals, as do Horgan's later works about "three races in the writings of four hundred years," a sympathy for common humanity and the places of its living. It is partially for this reason that biography figures so prominently in Horgan's conception of history and that the sense of spirit of place, of regionalism, is so strong. In *Chronicle* one can see the beginnings of Horgan's preoccupation with such great southwesterners as Gregg, Kearny, Lamy, and others and the landscape that gave their lives and actions meaning.

If *Chronicle* represents an important early attempt by Horgan to clarify and adjust his own view of history and his methodology as a historian in the tradition of Turner and Parkman, it also represents a more contemporary influence and an early lesson with another lesser-known historian, Maurice Garland Fulton, whose baggy pants, dusty books, and affection for cats seem today as endearing as they do quirky and stereotypically eccentric.

New Mexico's Own Chronicle, revisited in the light of Horgan's long and illustrious career and Fulton's dire-straits death just a year after Horgan's first Pulitzer Prize for history, remains, beyond the fiftieth anniversary of its publication, a monument to the chances of history that brought these two New Mexico writers together and made them, as individuals, a small part of the very history, the very chronicle to which, in its telling, they devoted so much of their lives and sensibilities.

Calculating the Distance

The obvious quality of distance is physical—the distance measurable between two points. More important for Willa Cather's artistry and her grasp of the passions of human life is a moral distance—the span between ignorance and awareness; between hope and bitter denial; between the civilization within a soul and whatever corroding condition would work to destroy it in hatred or, worse, indifference.
—Paul Horgan, "Willa Cather's Incalculable Distance"

THERE IS MUCH OF WILLA CATHER in the writings of Paul Horgan. There is, most obviously, their shared interest in Jean Baptiste Lamy and his life—an interest that for Cather provided motive for fiction and *Death Comes for the Archbishop* (1927); an interest that for Horgan culminated in his Pulitzer Price–winning history/biography, *Lamy of Santa Fe* (1975), although Lamy and his friend and fellow cleric, Joseph Machebeuf, also provided Horgan with material for diverse excursions into other narrative forms, including fiction.

The distance between Cather's *Archbishop* and Horgan's *Lamy*, however, is much less than the fifty-two-year span between these two books' publication dates might suggest. Calculating the distance between Cather's and Horgan's sensibilities as artists reveals considerable closeness, a kinship going beyond biography and aesthetic sensibility to include subject, setting, theme, and technique. Their respective styles, however, are distinctly their own.

Cather's style remains inimitable—the stuff of plain yet lyrical transcendence. Horgan's style, and his reputation as a writer's writer, is unique and bears his own individual imprint. He has been for over three-quarters of a century a person in love with books and words and writing—as a librarian and author. He is, moreover, an amateur musician and painter of considerable talent. So any tracing of influences on him would be a monumental if not an impossible effort and would reveal, finally, an eclectic range of literary and artistic progenitors. Beyond that are Horgan's talent and genius. Even so, there is in Horgan a considerable closeness with Cather—a closeness worth attempting to calculate. Their kinship revolves around their mutual devotion to the efficacy of the right word in the right place, at the right time; a mutual devotion to style.

Cather's influence on Horgan can be seen most obviously in Horgan's short fiction collected in *The Peach Stone: Stories from Four Decades (1967)*. But noteworthy too are Horgan's more explicit prose commentaries on Cather. His essay, "Willa Cather's Incalculable Distance" ("WCID"), found in his collection *A Certain Climate: Essays in History, Arts, and Letters,* provides a beginning.[1] Horgan wrote the essay in draft form for a speech before the Century Association, April 25, 1978. That speech remained unpublished until 1988—a decade's distance, which brought considerable revision to Horgan's original speech. Horgan also spoke on Cather in 1977 at the University of Notre Dame (one year after receiving the Pulitzer Prize for *Lamy*), where he helped dedicate a large bequest collection to the university's library. On that occasion he observed, "Many lectures have been given on Willa Cather, the Nebraskan who shared my love for the American Southwest. . . . When an author really has quality, there's always something new to be said about her or him."[2]

Horgan's respect for Cather also gains expression in his "Preface to an Unwritten Book," which appeared in the *Yale Review* in 1976, as well as in another speech/essay, "The Pleasures and Perils of Regionalism," given as an acceptance speech for a Distinguished Achievement Award from the Western Literature Association in Austin in 1973, and published in *Western American Literature* the following year. Yet another essay, which appeared in the *Catholic Historical Review* in 1961, "In Search of the Archbishop," also pays much homage to Cather.[3]

The aesthetic and historical processes outlined in all of Horgan's

Willa Cather writings reveal not just his continuing and sustained regard for her as an artist, but also reflect his own attempts to cross personal and professional "distance." They reveal, in sum, his expression of gratitude for Cather's presence and art.

Horgan's lectures on Cather in the 1960s and 1970s that culminated in "Willa Cather and the Incalculable Distance" stress her personal "search for her own inner as well as outer distance in her early life, until she finally found it in the writing of her novels and stories," a search, Horgan observes, wherein Cather "again and again . . . made that same search the deep concern of her fictional people," ("WCID," 86–87). Horgan shares a similar concern for his own fictive characters. Both in his early lecture on Cather and in his revised essay, Horgan stresses that Cather's incalculable distance is not merely the physical distance between two "points" (the original lecture manuscript says two "places"), but a "moral distance the span [says Horgan] between ignorance and awareness; between hope and bitter denial; between the civilization within a soul and whatever corroding condition would work to destroy it in hatred, or worse, indifference," ("WCID," 85–86).

This "moral distance" in Cather, according to Horgan, is a closure, an identity, a persona that seemed to identify for Cather whether or not we like a particular writer—the kind of concern Walker Gibson and Wayne Booth refer to as a reader identification of an "implied" writer, or the implied or "mock" reader. In his accounting of Cather's own "moral distance," Horgan quotes what she said about a reader's relationship with a writer: "We like a writer . . . much as we like individuals, for what he is, simply, underneath his accomplishments. Oftener than not, it is for some moral quality, some ideal which he himself cherishes, though it may be little discernible in his behavior in the world. It is the light behind his books, and it is the living quality of his sentences" ("WCID," 86).

In Horgan's tallying, Cather's fictive counterpart, Lucy Gayheart, like Cather herself, traveled from small-town Nebraska to Chicago to hear a great singer's recital—an "incalculable distance . . . from the wintry country and homely neighbors, to the city where the air trembled like a tuning fork with unimaginable possibilities," ("WCID,"

85). It is a distance which Horgan labels "aspiration," "humility before the greatest of human works," "delight so keen in the established justice of a truly achieved work of art that no pang is too much to suffer if only it can be felt" (WCID," 85). It is an ambition and a delight which Horgan sees prevailing, as well, in Cather's short story, "A Wagner Matinee." It is a journey and a distance covered "between ignorance and awareness; between hope and bitter denial," and away from hatred and indifference toward a humanistic love which Horgan charts in his own life and in his works of biography, history, and fiction.

It is, moreover, worth noting that Horgan's own development as an artist (from birth in Buffalo, New York in 1903; through boyhood in New Mexico, beginning with the family move to Albuquerque in 1915, including his time in Roswell as a cadet from 1919 to 1923 and on the faculty at New Mexico Military Institute after World War II; and continuing to his return to the East, to Wesleyan University and Connecticut, where he has resided since 1962) roughly parallels Cather's peregrinations. In all of Horgan's migrations, writer-East, writer-West, writer-East, each of which marks a phase in his career as author, he matched Cather's East-West moves from Virginia to Nebraska, and from Nebraska back east to Pittsburgh and New York, with sojourns in the Southwest. Like Cather, Horgan searched for culture and literacy, aspiration and hope, while he was (at least at first) estranged from the "garden" in a Southwest still awaiting discovery and "cultivation"—albeit in vaster, more sublime environs than Cather's first West, the Middle West of Nebraska.[4] It's no wonder that Lamy's gardening of the West appealed to both Cather and Horgan and provided an "objective correlative," of sorts, for their own histories.[5] On balance, Cather remains much more the southwestern tourist than Horgan, though he too was essentially eastern in his sensibilities (in correspondence, Harvey Fergusson, a writer Horgan much admired, regarded him as something of an "indoor boy"). Although he lived in New Mexico a number of years, and visited yearly for many subsequent years, Horgan needed the amenities of high culture, and returned to permanent residence in Connecticut, closer to his native New York.

In his account of his own encounters with the presence of Lamy in Santa Fe, Horgan relates that as a boy, soon after moving to New Mexico, beginning about 1915, he spent summers in Santa Fe. Although he noted the architectural revival styles of "pueblo" and "Santa Fe," "it was a French nineteenth-century air, [which] seemed to [him] the most *characterizing* element in Santa Fe," ("Archbishop," 411).

That influence was Lamy's Cathedral of St. Francis, the Mansard roof of St. Michael's College, the Gothic chapel of the Loretto Convent, and the porches of St. Vincent's Hospital. The distance to Lamy and French culture, as represented through such buildings and "spirit," was much closer and more impressive to Horgan than the indigenous adobe buildings. In Horgan's words, "These [nineteenth-century French styles] were the most prominent buildings, and in my youthful impression, they stood forth more importantly than the hillsides and lanes where small adobe houses sheltered most of the population—such houses as were called warrens for prairie dogs by early American travellers from the prairies, and as would in the twentieth century provide a whole new aesthetic in architecture for later settlers with developed sensibilities" ("Archbishop," 411). In stories told by friends who had known Lamy, and in the atmosphere of Santa Fe itself, Horgan identified with Lamy—and, by implication, with the ways in which the archbishop had closed the distance between France and New Mexico with his buildings and his gardens. Horgan explains Lamy's inspiring influence on his artistic and literary aspirations this way: "When I went to the cathedral at Santa Fe, or walked along the long wall of the Bishop's Garden, or heard the Angelus clapping its rings of sound over the city, he was somewhere behind my thought, my eye, my ear, and one day he would move me to vest him, however poorly, in my word" ("Archbishop," 412).

If Lamy and his influence characterized Santa Fe for Horgan and Cather, so too did Horgan identify Cather with Lamy and the City of Faith. Horgan's account of how, one summer morning in 1926 in the La Fonda Hotel (Horgan was twenty-three), Lamy and Cather and Santa Fe all converged for him, has something of the air of legend about it. If not exactly a mythic meeting then it was surely a

Wordsworthian "spot of time" of fateful proportions, an encounter that both directly and indirectly influenced Horgan as person and as author.

Horgan infuses the convergence with drama and novelistic flourish and imagination, describing how Cather was busily working on a porch of the La Fonda Hotel, and how his interruption bothered her. In his devotion, he quickly left without saying a word.

Horgan's first published short story, "The Head of the House of Wattleman," appeared in the *Yale Review* three years later, after that chance encounter. Other short stories and narratives followed. His first published novel, *The Fault of Angels,* which won the Harper Prize novel contest, appeared seven years later—in 1933. It was the first of a long succession of successful novels. Clearly Horgan's brush with Cather—as esteemed author—did much to motivate his own identification not just with Lamy but with the author's life. This linkage, this closeness with Cather's method of work and urgency, presented in almost heroic proportions, is apparent in Horgan's assessment of seeing the great lady: "Decades later, and myself the victim of countless interruptions of my own working situations, I know acutely what it may have cost Miss Cather to recover through deep breaths of mind that wonderful, removed, beautifully lost sense of utmost communion with one's subject which every artist must develop for himself every time he works, and which I had shattered for her" ("Archbishop," 413).

Cather's own closeness to her work, which Horgan knows he interrupted, is known precisely because of his subsequent closeness as an artist with his subject. Unintended though her intrusion was on young Horgan as would-be writer, Cather imprinted him greatly for there is little doubt that he bonded with her in a way similar to his identification with Lamy. Horgan wants to believe, and infers, that Cather too was preoccupied with the archbishop that day at the La Fonda.

Horgan makes clear that during the next several years, after he had authored ten or twelve books, Cather's novel on Lamy still "presented . . . immediate and wonderfully vague and strongly potential notions for a work about him [Lamy] in another form than the novel" ("Archbishop," 414). Horgan's retracing of his convergence with Lamy and Cather in Santa Fe is, moreover, something of a repeat, doubling performance of Cather's own account of how she came to write *Death Comes for the Archbishop*,[6] and so the distance between Cather and Horgan diminishes on yet another level. It is not too farfetched to surmise that other aspects of Cather's art, beyond sensibility into technique, were also imprinted Horgan. He clearly presents himself as a student before her work.

In "Preface to an Unwritten Book," he wrote that he began reading Cather as a student at Albuquerque High when Cather's sister, who taught freshman English, introduced him to her sister's books ("Preface," 324). This early reading under the pedagogical tutelage of Elsie Cather and the master novelist's "example" is no small consideration in calculating the distance between Cather as mentor and novelist and Horgan as student and novelist, between Cather as novelist and Horgan as novelist and historian. And it helps one understand how all of Horgan's biographies and histories evidence strong narrative and fictional techniques—including recreating a scene through imagination beyond absolutely verifiable fact, to dialogue and imagistic and descriptive enhancement of setting, character, and plot.

Whatever calculations Cather and Horgan made about the Southwest and its distances, its lives and landscapes, there is little doubt that the magnet and the prism of the East affected the perceptions of both writers, their "tallies" and measuring of distances, aesthetic and geographical.[7] In his commentary on three of Cather's stories, "The Sculptor's Funeral," "A Death in the Desert," and "A Wagner Matinee," Horgan hits hard on the theme of western artistic and physical isolation and exile, a theme common in his own stories as well. It is a persona, a stance which Horgan himself assumed, whether visiting in the artist colony of Santa Fe or working devotedly on his first writings in the remote New Mexico town of Roswell—a town where John McGinnis, Walter Prescott Webb, and J. Frank Dobie sought him out as a key contributor to the Southwest Renaissance, and a town which he worked hard to cultivate through helping establish a museum.

Horgan observes that if Cather's treatments of exiles seem to lack full sympathy "for helpless states of uninformed life," they do work as portraits which "risk seeming over-fastidious . . . the fact remains that great contrasts in cultural ways naturally call forth personal choices—or at least should afford the opportunity to choose" ("Preface," 324). Time and again Horgan's characters choose, like Cather's, to aspire to resist "deracination," to replace philistinism with sophistication, to close the distance not just between high culture and low, but between East and West. Horgan has little tolerance for "regionalism" in any delimiting sense and regards himself as a transcontinental author. His essay on "The Pleasures and Perils of Regionalism" reads, as do all of his Cather writings, like an indictment of self-conscious, stylized, commercialized "placeness."

His is a warning not to exploit regional differences and styles for mercenary means. Cather succeeds as an artist of region, of West, for Horgan, because in her fiction she responded more or less incidentally to locale. "It is her lively artistry which holds us for its own sake—how things are said, rather more than what they are about" ("P&P," 170).

Here resides one of the key considerations in calculating the closeness of Cather and Horgan—the issue of style. Horgan appears to hold that style is identifiable with "how things are said, rather more than what they are about," with the language itself rather than with just its content. And so it would seem with Cather in her allegiance to the "unfurnished" novel, in her recognition of what could be felt on the page without being named. And that is, paradoxically, the basis of the "incalculable distance" in both Horgan and Cather and between them. It is what contributes to their ultimate proximity—the striving of style to transcend place and plot, setting, character, and theme. It is an assumption that is, for some, refuted in Horgan's and in Cather's writings. However difficult to define, and however nebulous, style is the means by which the distance between all great writers is finally calculated and their kinship established or denied.

And "style" is why Horgan, while influenced by Cather and a kindred spirit to her, is much more than her imitator. Horgan would have been a writer, an artist of some kind, even if he had never seen Cather or read her works. But chances are that he would not have been so great a writer as he has remained all these years, if he had not interrupted her at her work on the porch of the La Fonda, in the very royal and rich, beautiful and legendary city of Santa Fe, one-time Spanish capital of Nueva Granada, and still a spiritual and cultural nodality of the great American Southwest.

Legacy: The Great Literatus

The great literatus will be known, among the rest, by his cheerful sim-plicity, his adherence to natural standards, his limitless faith in God, his reverence, and by the absence in him of doubt, ennui, burlesque, per-siflage, or any strain'd and temporary fashion.

— *Walt Whitman,* A National Literature

IN HIS EXUBERANT ACCOUNTING of "A National Literature," won-derful and wondrous Walt Whitman established some esteemed cri-teria for the nation's "great literatus": "cheerful simplicity," "adher-ence to natural standards," "limitless faith in God," "reverence," and "the absence . . . of doubt, ennui, burlesque, persiflage, or any strain'd and temporary fashion."[1]

Whitman knew his times and knew himself and throughout all his prophetic singing he looms large as his own great literatus; his own strong, multitudinous voicings always striving, "simmering, simmering" for the democratic, the American ideal. His own great-ness is always somewhere found in his proclamations of promise and in his queries. "Where," he asks, during the "stormiest passions of history" which were crossing his day, "where is the man of letters, where is the book, with any bolder aim than to follow in the old track, repeat what has been said before—and, as its utmost triumph, sell well . . . ?"[2]

Whitman's ego, his exuberant personae and presence and attain-ment, do not, however, overshadow or cancel out his announced standards for the arrival of the great American literatus, the great American writers to come after him.

Whitman, like Emerson before him, knew well that there is not "One Man," rather "he is all."[3] Today, however, the great literatus, the American Scholar, the woman or man of nature, spirit, thought, and of action, needs to be even more inclusive, more varied, more multidimensional—in proportion to the amplified passions of history crossing our lives and culture; more encompassing, greater than Whitman and Emerson and their prophetic company could begin to glimpse.

As great writers they were, however, prescient in their assumptions and attitudes. They were prophetic in their encompassing dispositions. In their time they anticipated what (in our time of deconstruction, gender analysis, feminism, masculinism, Paleface-Redskin dichotomies; this centrism and that integrative, interdisciplinary study; the New Journalism, the New History, the New Ethnicity; multiculturalism, and other revisionist stances toward historical process and canonization) is in our time regarded as a "thicker," and "deeper," more richly textured and complex appraisal of greatness and quality, of truth and beauty.

Today, many readers and perhaps most critics question the very assumptions that presuppose any such philosophical and aesthetic absolutes, any "great" attainment.

So, to consider Paul Horgan, his Southwest, his *Nueva Granada* and his literary legacy for twentieth-century, modern, contemporary, postcontemporary, present-day and the abiding, mythic *Aztlán,* of Mexican-American demarcation, is a large order. For to consider Horgan's enduring value as an American writer—a person I surely regard as a great literatus in Whitman's terms—is to attempt to reconcile Horgan's "great" achievement with the provocative and at times compelling questioning of not only the need but even the very possibility of achieving what Horgan has long sought: greatness, quality, or as Horgan terms it, "the elite."

"Man of letters," "regionalist," "humanist," all of the designations that discussions of Horgan have so easily adopted in the past, must now accommodate new approaches to history and to literature, if his great art and sensibility, his great heart and spirit as a historian, biographer, fictionist, and as an essayist, are truly to endure—not just in the academy (where, alas, he has never really found total favor, never been regarded and accepted as *à la mode*), and not just as a writer's writer (which he most certainly is), but in the great pulse and mind of the common reader.

For it is arguable that not in spite of his eloquence but because of it, Horgan's own best home, his own most lasting legacy is precisely in the "common heart," as he once phrased it. His gift to us is in his sustained and consistently high artistic performance as what he prefers to think of as a "maker," spanning most of this curious and tumultuous current century.

Lest anybody relegate him to old-fashioned fuddyduddydom or the now often disdained shelves of Anglo-European or sexist irrelevance, it must be asserted that Horgan, first as part of the Southwestern Renaissance, in which the state of Texas and Southern Methodist University can claim large stake, in his many novels and short stories, and in his two great Pulitzer Prize–winning works of history and biography—in all these ways it must be said that he was in the vanguard of wanting to see. And according to his own best lights he sees not just the Turnerian East-West dynamics of national settlement, but the South-Southwest cultural and geographical vectors which now are viewed as defining not only the ethnicity, the culture of life in the Southwest, but the American, the U.S., the "us" experience.

Horgan too, it should be attested, was similarly in the vanguard of seeing the many ethnic and cultural laminations which define, again, not just the American Indian/Mexican-American/Anglo-American Southwest but multicultural American experiences. Always greatly empathetic with the experiences of women—in the West, in the East, and across the continent—Horgan should be credited too for realistically and sincerely going beyond any doctrinaire or patronizing portrayal of women. A consideration of the images of women in Horgan's writings should prove affirming to feminist readers of either gender—as should his compassion for the various attractions and antagonisms of human sexuality.

Moreover, when it comes to accommodating and integrating the techniques and methodologies of narration—fictive and nonfictive, historical and novelistic—Horgan should be acknowledged as one of the century's masters of the truth of art, of truths going beyond mere fact and reportage while never distorting "fact," insofar as it was determinable. And throughout all of his writings Horgan should also be judged a supreme stylist—merging and blending content with structure; never attempting style for style's sake, devoid of meaning or value, as a mere condiment (notwithstanding occasional accusations of affectation, of just "prettiness" in lieu of "history"). Furthermore, his religious devotion, his passion and purpose in affirming man, God, and the religious spirit infuse and inform each of Horgan's books, each of his essays, each of his letters.

Horgan's own words illuminate some of his attitudes toward the kind of Whitmanesque inclusivity outlined above. Here is Horgan on the interrelationships between history and literature, fiction and nonfiction:

> There are of course many phases of history, biography and even techniques of fiction, which cloud over each other. Separation of these is difficult. History, the chronicle of past times, cannot be told except through the events of human life. Biography cannot be richly set forth unless the backgrounds and social atmosphere of the subject are evoked. The forward impulsion of a chronicle can often be beautifully served by the instrument of narrative as used by a competent novelist. Further, the resources of the literary artist—sense of form, eye for detail, mastery of proportion, intuition of human nature, delight in environment, and above all a gift for breathing life into character—can properly be brought into the writing of history provided that historical truth, so far as the historian can determine it, is not violated. All works of historiography are subject to later revision as hitherto unavailable facts are unearthed. Honorably used in the service of historical truth, the devices of the literary artist provide the one constant in a work of history or biography in its time, until inevitably overtaken by revelations of continuing research. The "social scientist, the quantifier, and the statistician" bring their technical observations;

the literary artist brings his values; neither need exclude the other—indeed, cannot do so, if the gifts of each are unified in the person of the historian himself. It is such completeness we hope for, no matter how rarely we find it.[4]

And here is Horgan on style generally and his writing style particularly: "Oh, style is simply one's signature. Its perception by others surely must depend on their capacity to appreciate it. In any case, I mustn't complain when I am accused of literacy."[5] And listen to him comment, somewhat impatiently, on his interaction with landscape, nature and the out-of-doors:

> In your book on Harvey Fergusson [*Frontier's End: The Life and Literature of Harvey Fergusson,* Lincoln, 1989], you quote him; "Paul is an indoor boy." He was right, if he was comparing me to his own enacted ideal of the wilderness conqueror, the hunter, the self-measurer against tooth and talon, silence and solitude. But I have brought other values to "nature and outdoor settings." I have been much outdoors. My writing is often pictorial, even painterly; aspects which are not matured within walls. I have all my life greatly loved landscape, in all its physical components, and their profound effect upon human society and individual lives. No, I am not a "nature" writer, nor have I a message about the environment as such (and, indeed, I don't think I brandish "messages" of any sort in my work: certain values are perhaps to be discerned there by the discerning). I would patiently add that the ecology of the drawing room is quite as valid in the way of literary material as any other environment in which human beings find themselves.[6]

Seldom, then, among twentieth-century writers, U.S. writers, regional writers, southwestern writers, are such talents and attainments combined and reconciled in one great, enduring writer, a true person of letters and polymath. Always true to his own heart, his own consonant sympathies with the common heart of humanity, with lives and landscapes and their respective communing spirits of moment and place, Paul Horgan is surely now identifiable and will continue to be known "among the rest," as Whitman's, as our great literatus. For this, and for this wonderful collection of his works, we pay him tribute, well knowing, that as libraries, East and West, and his many readers across the country attest, past, passing, and to come, his books are his own best monument, his own America, his Southwest and, gratefully, ours.

The Centuries of Santa Fe: A New Perspective

MOST PEOPLE MOLD THE AMERICAN WEST, and especially an exotic and magical town such as Santa Fe, New Mexico, into their own mind's and heart's making. Paul Horgan is no exception.

The history one finds in Horgan's writings is always influenced by the truths of fiction. His Pulitzer Price—winning works, *Great River* (1954) and *Lamy of Santa Fe* (1975), are as much biography as history, as much novels as nonfiction narratives.

In *The Centuries of Santa Fe* (first published in 1956), Horgan's panoramic history of the City of Faith from its founding by the Spanish in 1610 through three centuries of subsequent Mexican and Yankee domination, his sensibilities, his assumptions, yes, even his biases fill every page of this now classic "history/story" of one of our nation's most ancient, historic, and legendary cities.

Horgan would never have believed it, and is probably still aghast to find that *The Centuries of Santa Fe*, albeit beautiful and true, both aesthetic and accurate, in its own way, is today a rather controversial book, viewed as a classic case of the kind of history that needs to be reconsidered, reperceived and, many would argue, rectified.

To say this is, of course, to assume that history, both its "facts" and its interpretation, is relative—to hold that truth, like beauty, depends on its beholder. It is an attitude about historiography which would not bring Horgan's full agreement because he appeals generally to a more categorical, absolutist belief in "historical fact."

It is, nevertheless, difficult, in any context, to determine just how much of history exists outside any given historian's or any school of historians' accounting of it. Most would agree that when history is written by a novelist, the issue becomes even more problematic. And over the six or so decades of his life as a professional writer Horgan has time and again encountered the question asked in the *New Yorker* by Stanley Walker about *Great River*, "Pretty, but is it history?"

New Mexico historian Frank D. Reeve in his own "Letter to Clio" in the *New Mexico Historical Review* (April, 1956) echoed Walker's sentiments by classifying Horgan as an amateur historian. (Horgan, not Reeve, won the Pulitzer prizes!) And no less a Santa Fean than Oliver La Farge, in his comments on *Centuries* in the *New York Times Book Review* (Oct. 7, 1956) conceded that although Horgan had researched his obscure archival material well, and complimented him for doing so, the result—thought La Farge—was compromised by the somewhat rankling realization that Horgan had never really established his credentials, attained a true kinship with or settled in Santa Fe because "he is much too formal a dresser." Horgan and more cosmopolitan kindred spirits like the late Wallace Stegner would counter that one needn't traipse around in turquoise jewelry, Levis, or boots of bizarre leathers to write authentically about Santa Fe or the West.

A comment about *Centuries* (*Saturday Review*, Dec. 8, 1956) revealing some quirky curmudgeonry was that of Texas historian Walter Prescott Webb: "Paul Horgan is one of an increasing group of fiction writers and artists who are drifting into the field of history, bringing with them a good deal of their literary baggage. . . . This effort to combine the gold of literature with the silver of history is hazardous and may result in something that conveys the impression of costume jewelry."

Clearly historians, amidst their personal rivalries and professional jealousies, assume a variety of things about the nature of history and the writing about it. Artists perceive "history" and interpret it just as variously. As a result, especially when seen through the reperceptions of the 1990s, more and more we are coming into even greater realizations that there were and are many Wests, real and imagined. And many Wests imagined as "real."

Horgan was not a revisionist historian in the 1950s when he wrote *Great River* and *Centuries*—nor is he today any more of a revisionist or relativist, any more *à la mode* as he approaches his own century mark. He stands firm in his dedication to elitist standards of choice and quality, as he sees them. He eschews fashion for fashion's sake, insisting that if he cared to, he could be as *à la mode* as any best-selling author.

Horgan was not, when he moved from Buffalo, New York, to New Mexico as a boy—and he is not today, in his Middletown, Connecticut, residence—in his heart and soul a true westerner. As a product of his era and his class, Horgan adopted much of the technique and much of the attitude of historians such as Francis Parkman and Frederick Jackson Turner, both of whom saw French, Spanish, and English incursions into the relatively innocent North American continent and the eradication or forced colonization of its indigenous inhabitants as inevitable and just—as "progress" and as "manifest," "civilizing" destiny.

This is not to say that Horgan is boorishly insensitive to American Indians and Mexican Americans. As attested in contemplated reissues of *The Habit of Empire* (1939), his account of Don Vicente Zaldivar's attack on Acoma Pueblo in 1599, and published in notes to readers in *The Thin Mountain Air* (1977), the last volume of his Richard trilogy, Horgan has offered some explanations and justifications of his early portrayals of American Indians and Mexican Americans.

As a result of Horgan's nineteenth-century orientations, *The Centuries of Santa Fe* seems rather Victorian (albeit stylistically beautiful, even breathtakingly lyrical and poetic in places) in its doctrinaire Anglo-European and "elitist" vantage points, almost quaint when held up to the hard-hitting, questioning, and protesting historians of the New West, the New Ethnicity, the New History.

Curiously, however, therein lies the book's continuing and enduring value as a southwestern classic in an atomized age when the very existence of "classics" and of a monoculture is questioned and held accountable, often in the most agitated and angriest of ways.

This state of affairs—diverse ethnic centrism and separatism—needless to say, Horgan laments and sees as subversive to the national motto of *e pluribus unum*, a motto to which he fervently subscribes. Be that as it may, in today's cultural climate, what one century sees and knows as givens, as constants, as "facts" are the stuff, ironically, only of the constancies of change, of mutability, of knowledge become, ultimately, inevitably, naive if not vain. What one ethnic group, one gender, social class, or occupational group sees and knows as "truth" is actually their truth, their perception of what happened, is happening, or will happen.

Persons of all persuasions must now, in this most wondrous of information ages, fully comprehend that history can't be told from all of the possible points of view—whether human or geological or ecological. Perhaps film or "virtual reality," or some other less linear means and medium than a book (even an intentionally encompassing book such as *Centuries*), will one day capture the great and varied simultaneity of history, of individual and collective human experience. Perhaps not—as any single individual's relatively confined but enormously complex daily calendar or biographical life map would seem to suggest.

What were the lives really like of the purportedly ordinary yet stereotypic individuals Horgan both invents and chronicles: the royal notary, the bannerman, the alderman, the matriarch, the Missouri trader, the United States lieutenant, the German bride, the doctor of medicine? And were these ordinary heroes and heroines really as humanly and benevolently treated by the historical greats whom Horgan recreates in his staging of their intersecting, romanticized lives? And what of the anonymous "heroes" and masses of humanity we only glimpse around the margins, in the background of *Centuries*?

In such queries the familiar questions of fairness and hindsight soon arise. If the endless variations of history are impossible to represent and record, why expect Horgan as historian to do it? Why expect a certain kind of writer of history, in Horgan's case a novelistic, narrative historian, to do it? And, perhaps most unfair of all applications of such assumptions about the imperative "relativity of otherness," why criticize Horgan (as mortal scribe at the moment of and in the act of writing), who had little benefit of either vast and various racial memories, common hindsight, or crystal-ball prescience?

These are surrounding and salient questions to ask when reading *The Centuries of Santa Fe* today. What will hit most contemporary readers of Horgan's history is how, almost in spite of himself, he ostensibly advances an ambivalent interpretation of Santa Fe, and, by implication, of the Southwest and of United States history, which is actually and decidedly ethnocentric, sweepingly Anglo-European, male, and Catholic in its orientation.

This is, however, precisely why *Centuries* needs to be read again now as the twentieth turns into the twenty-first century. Horgan is a quintessential exemplar of such a conservative but passing world view. Few could present it more sincerely, more passionately, and, it now becomes increasingly apparent, make it more nostalgically beautiful and romantic than does Horgan.

Is Horgan's Santa Fe the real Santa Fe through the ages? Hardly. For what is the "real" Santa Fe? Spanish colony? Mercantile mecca? Mexican outpost? American garrison? Tourist trap? Artists' sanctuary? Celebrity hangout? Namesake for stylized curio hype?

Where does history merge with legend? Where do stereotype and caricature supercede archetype and character? Were Juan de Oñate and Don Diego de Vargas, Josiah Gregg, Archbishop Lamy, Adolph Bandelier, General Stephen Watts Kearny, and Kit Carson, along with all of the "types" that were part of their historic entourage, their cavalcade of history—were these replicated personages the at once ordinary and exceptional "heroes" Horgan makes them out to be?

More importantly, are Horgan's heroes ours? Were Spanish and American militarism and imperialism and male dominance and control in all forms of civil and domestic governance quite as pleasurable and desirable and accommodating as Horgan generally portrays them? If they were, should they have been? Are they now so perceived?

Consider, for example, the irony of the following passage from *Centuries* (made by Horgan himself in the *coda* persona of "Chronicler") when read against the background of the present-day allegations of sexual misconduct and the resultant scandal that brought about the recent resignation of New Mexico's Archbishop Robert

Sanchez: "The sense of Archbishop Lamy and all his works still reaches over Santa Fe today like a blessing. The religion which he restored in New Mexico retains its dignity and humble universality."

At the time of Lamy's church reforms and rule, and today, not everybody sees the Catholic presence in Santa Fe in as sanguine a light as does Horgan in *Centuries*. Chicano historian Ray John de Aragon, for example, disavows Lamy as a benefactor. But the value of Horgan's partisan history is that it reinforces not only the relativity of history but the fickleness of fate and the futility of sweeping projections about legacies. And this contributes to the inevitable dialectic that ensues from a contemporary reading of *Centuries*.

Were the Pueblo Indians, especially those of Santo Domingo, Zuni, Acoma, and Isleta, quite the "children of the Sun" replicated here? Were the Indians of Taos Pueblo, the Navajos, the Apaches, and the Comanches quite as unjustifiably "savage" in their initial resistance to and sporadic rebellion against conquest? Should Popé be relegated to a sentence for his role in the 1680 Pueblo uprising? American Indian historians Alfonso Ortiz and Joe Sando, to name two, are convincing in their appeals for indigenous, "other-side" interpretations of Spanish and American settlement. Their histories of a newer ethnicity, their revisionist, "underside" perspectives, thicken rather than nullify Horgan's perspectives, Horgan's histories. History reflecting such a dialectic takes on the fuller meaning of tensions, speculations, and various "truths."

Perhaps the most striking instance of novelistic indulgence or poetic license in the book is Horgan's account of "The German Bride: 1870." Here, in effect, he fuses the history of Albuquerque with that of Santa Fe, showing again that he is interested most in types and in essences. Most of this account follows the actual biography of Albuquerque's early merchant founder, Franz Huning, and the building of his house known as Huning Castle, and his Old Town mercantile business—and the importation of his German bride and his German architectural tastes. Not coincidentally, the German bride's Old World tastes are much in harmony with Bishop Lamy's attempts to build his Santa Fe cathedral in the fashions of his native France.

Is Horgan's Santa Fe real? Is Santa Fe Albuquerque? Is New Mexico *Nueva Granada,* Spain, Mexico, Germany, or France? *The Centuries of Santa Fe* seems to want to tell us so. Authors know certain truths. Readers know others. We all readily perceive and create our real and willed worlds. And Santa Fe, that great and ultimately inscrutable City of Faith, knows truths of its own.

Santa Fe, vibrant and pulsating and magnetic, like all great cities, like history itself, is ever-changing—anything but static. Some, like Paul Horgan, may prefer to think of it, in all its panorama of great personages and anonymous stereotypical humanity, as a Royal City, even an eternal city much in the shadow of Rome or of Jamestown, a city of Christian, Catholic verities. But when reading and reconsidering *The Centuries of Santa Fe* on the cusp of yet another century—at once marvelous in potential and brimming with peril—it behooves all serious readers, even the most devoted of Horgan's fans and friends, to pause and reflect on the putative historical and cultural, as well as the spiritual and aesthetic "certainties" of Santa Fe. They are hard-won and hard-lost certainties, as various and as vaguely knowable as history itself—concepts of the human mind, of time, of space, of what is past, passing, and to come.

Another great poet-historian, albeit of a more guilt-ridden persuasion, William Carlos Williams, in his own classic work of American history and biography, *In the American Grain* (1925), reminds us of how ephemeral "facts" are in their historical fragility: "History, history! We fools, what do we know or care? History begins for us with murder and enslavement, not with discovery." If tempered and read against such awareness of the relativity of history and of historical perspective, *The Centuries of Santa Fe* remains, in its sincere, dedicated faith and special "truths" both a beautiful and rich book. And for this all readers, in the tourism of their mortality, in momentary contemplation of the riddle of Santa Fe, are indebted to Paul Horgan, a historian and artist hero of great occasion.

Completive Polarities: Interview

When they come back to him as they still occasionally do, he wonders if he listens to them in memory, as if to hear the dialog of body and soul? Heart and mind? The dialog of life between its completive polarities. Let us listen to hear the voices . . .
—*Paul Horgan,* Whitewater

I FIRST INTERVIEWED PAUL HORGAN at his home in Middletown, Connecticut. I spent two days talking with Mr. Horgan, and he was gracious to my intrusions in every way. The first interview, which turned out to be a rather long one, took place in the summer of 1979, and the information gathered there served as a basis for my subsequent book, *Paul Horgan,* published by G. K. Hall in 1983. The discussions took place over coffee in his home, a converted carriage house on the Wesleyan University campus. As we talked, Mr. Horgan would leave off petting his cat—who sat contentedly in Mr. Horgan's lap for much of the time—to reach for a book on one of his many amply loaded bookshelves, or a piece of informative material, perhaps a letter or a note or a manuscript page from his writing desk, which was situated in the corner of the large study and library where we talked. At strategic times we would break for refreshment, and at noon we headed off for a nice lunch at one of his favorite local restaurants. I remember being much impressed with not only what Mr. Horgan said but with his easy eloquence and quick wit. All of his many experiences and all of his many illustrious friends which he discussed came to life for me in quite transforming ways, for I was seeing for the first time in my life how a great living author lived and worked. Although this particular interview is nearly twenty years in the past, it is as vivid and as exciting to me still as if it were last week. It is my hope that the reader will share in my enjoyment and my enlightenment in hearing Mr. Horgan talk about his craft, his own great artistry, and his fervent dedication to his calling as a "maker."

*

RG: How about influences? Cather? Fergusson?—D. H. Lawrence? You wrote a story about Lawrence. Did you ever meet D. H. Lawrence?

PH: I never met him. I can't brag about that. My friend Witter Bynner, the poet in Santa Fe, knew him very well, and wrote I think best about him of anyone that ever has. A book called *Journey with Genius,* a wonderful book by Bynner, about his trip to Mexico with Lawrence and Frieda. Well, the *Southwest Review* published this one little story called, I think, "So Little Freedom," (which I reprinted in *The Peach Stone*) and Bynner read it and said, "It's the best portrait of Lawrence that's ever been written," and I never met him. He said, "It's exactly like the man." That pleased me very much.

I just missed him by a year. I became great friends later with Mrs. Lawrence. And liked her very much, very warm in a roly-poly, comic kind of way. I'm sorry I never saw him. I have restrained admiration for Lawrence, I must say. He's the kind of undisciplined writer that I don't find very much in. He has strokes, naturally, of power and at times even genius. But on the whole I don't think that he's a good writer.

RG: Anything else about writers and influences?

PH: No. That's been asked often. And I've scratched my brain over this. I can't put my finger on any direct influence on how I perform.

R G : You mention in *Approaches to Writing* that you were sort of off by yourself, developing in your own way.

P H : I still have to hold with that. I think that probably, again, because of my "accursed versatility" the influences all derived from observing and feeling for all the forms of the arts as they are not imitatable but analogous for the writer. I had lunch the other day at Amherst with Henry Steele Commanger. And I said that music was a perfectly marvelous analogy for the writer. "Oh, no, no, no!" he said, "it's fatuous to imitate." And I said not imitate! You cannot imitate musical form on the page. But certainly there are great analogies in musical structure, musical form which the writer can learn from. That's all I meant.

But in answer to your larger question, I think this is also true about how I see painting, how I hear music and how I feel about the theater, and what happens with character and what happens with such an element as dialog. But as to direct influences, . . . I have many loves, but I can't think that after that early period which I describe in *Approaches,* of conscious imitation, attempting to be successful in somebody else's clothes; I don't think, again, I did that.

R G : Lon Tinkle places you with the Southwestern Renaissance group. Even in *Approaches* you say there was a northern New Mexico school, Taos and Santa Fe.

P H : They were just residents. They weren't like each other. They really weren't. And I'm not like any other southwestern writer I know about.

R G : What did Tinkle mean by that?

P H : Well, there really was a Southwestern Renaissance. It didn't begin with me or with anybody in New Mexico. I think it began in Texas with John McGinnis, Professor McGinnis at SMU. You probably read the anecdote about it in *Approaches* . . . , he, driving [to Roswell] and driving all the way back after interviewing me. Incredible interview. He, driving all the way back! He was really an immense power. A remarkable man. He started the *Southwest Review* and began focusing . . . , he and Walter Webb and Dobie at the University in Austin.

At the same time, or perhaps a little earlier, I may be wrong in this, writers did begin to descend in flocks upon Santa Fe, as painters did. And that was part of the Renaissance. [C. P.] Snow . . . credits me with a . . . , well, as an interpreter of the Southwest who took a position . . . , and he thinks that there was something prophetic about my writing so, I suppose, he believes, so perceptively and deeply about it. Because now the Southwest is a very great area, known by everyone. And it wasn't then. It was a remote region. But I had no such conscious intention. He allows that—that perhaps it was an unconscious prophecy that I found so much in it to write about, to display, and to celebrate. But if I'm a part of the Southwestern Renaissance it is just because of time. It wasn't because of any association or any influence either way. I hadn't the smallest effect on anyone else, or they on me.

Actually the first serious New Mexico writer of modern times was Harvey Fergusson, a wonderful novelist who is dreadfully underestimated. . . . He's a remarkably fine writer.

R G : Bynner wasn't so much an influence as a friend?

P H : Just a friend. That's right. The Bynner Foundation has just published four volumes of his work. I was one of the executors. We published the Chinese poems, his own selected poems, the prose pieces, and satire and light verse. Volume five will be letters. But, again, I would say there was no influence there in a literary way. I would see him in Santa Fe frequently. One of my school mates at Roswell became his companion, and lived with him in Santa Fe for years. I would see him up in Santa Fe. They both appear in my book on Stravinsky.

R G : What do you think of [Robert] Craft's book on Stravinsky [*Stravinsky: The Chronicle of a Friendship*. New York: Alfred A. Knopf, 1972]?

P H : Oh, its wonderful. I'm having a wonderful time. It's very slow going because it's documentary. But Craft has knit things together. . . . Madame Stravinsky has been responsible for the translations from Russian and German. And also miles of materials. Monstrous. You'll have to spend an awful lot of time on it. But it will reward you, particularly if you have interest in him and the cultural period of the Russian ballet.

R G : Did you see her on the Dick Cavett show?

P H : Yes, I did. I could have killed Cavett. He kept interrupting. She'd get on an interesting line and he'd destroy her continuity. She's a very dear friend of mine.

R G : I enjoyed your book on Stravinsky very much. But I was reading it for your autobiography.

P H : Well, the first part, the original first part was infinitely longer. And it formed the frame of a certain period of my life in autobiography. But for purposes of this study it was out of proportion. So I narrowed it way down. I just kept it to those aspects of my life which he influenced.

R G : Do you intend to write your autobiography?

P H : Yes, one day. If I have the time. I have scads of work. . . . A terrific weight of stuff to deal with.

R G : How do you get it all done?

P H : Daily appointment, I guess.

R G : What else about your working habits? Inspiration?

P H : Inspirations are not dictatable and they can't be summoned. They just happen. They hit you. They are like being stung by an invisible insect. They come from all directions. At any time. Day or night. And they still keep coming. And they still make notes blossom. Some of the notes are productive, develop organically in a wonderful way. Others die and you don't know why. They all seem fascinating at the moment. Some don't have that power of further imaginative growth. And they disappear. But the ones that last eventually become something.

I'm right now (and this is in parenthesis) engaged in realizing many notes from many years that never die, for short stories. I've written fifty-two short stories in the last eighteen months. Various lengths. Don't be impressed. Because some are only a page long. They're true stories. Real stories. Some are quite long, thirty to forty pages. Some only ten to twelve pages. But these all were kernels that smote me at one time and still have power when I reconstruct them, and look at the notes. Some were notes of no power. That disposes of inspiration. You never know what will turn into something. I'm trying very hard to get to seventy stories and then stop, and let Bob Giroux pick a rather hefty volume out of it. But the trouble is I keep getting new notions for more stories. And I don't know when I'll finish. They keep happening.

R G : When do you find time to take your notes?

P H : At the instant. If something occurred to me right now I'd note it right now. I'd ask your permission and I'd write it down. And I've just sent eight notebooks to the Morgan Library in New York. That's another reference. . . . I sent them the original manuscript of *Approaches to Writing*, and both editions, paper and hardcover, and the notebooks from which the central portion is taken. They asked for something. It's the one time I broke my Beinecke rule. I love the Pierpont Morgan Library and I'm a life fellow there. I think it's the greatest museum in New York. Well, it's a library really.

R G : Where do you write at present?

P H : I write here. This is my library. That corner over there is where I work. That round table. The reference books are all there. I type. I use my handwriting and then I revise.

* *

R G : What about the issues of "regionalism," definitions and the like? You don't like to be considered a regionalist?

P H : Well, everybody's a regionalist. It can be expanded to everything. Tolstoy was a regionalist because he wrote about the places he knew. Where one is, where one lives. And what one lives is what one writes. In a sense it's an artificial concept. It's a handy concept, if you think of Hardy as a regionalist. But he's transcendent, so much more than "regionalist."

So I don't know how the vogue came into being. It was a phenomenon of the 1920s and '30s, I believe. I think it was given immense impetus by the government support of the arts in the terrible Depression days when artists were in a very bad way . . . and the government commisioned so much. And naturally to celebrate various parts of the country would be a good federal gesture and it would also conveniently tap the local talent. I think that's how regionalism got its vogue, so to speak. And then people got rather heavy about it and turned it into a philosophy. But if you take the philosophy far enough it just seems to evaporate. It seems to be fatuous to consider that there is a major justification for that kind of perception. It's just accidental.

R G : What about your semester at the University of Iowa? What was it, 1946?

P H : Yes, I came out of the army in January of 1946 and then went to Iowa City, to the Graduate School of Letters and the Writers Workshop headed by Paul Engle. I went there to teach and it seemed at the time a good bridge back from the cultural aridity of military life, though I had nothing but a profitable experience in the army. (I feel pretty good about being in the army and doing my duty there.) But I still needed to get back to my work bench as a writer. And I'm very glad I did. I loved the place . . . I own.

R G : Did you write anything there?

P H : Yes, the novel *Memories of the Future* [see later in interview]. In *The Distant Trumpet*, there's a little episode—rather a beautiful little episode, I think—in Galena, Illinois, from which trumpeter Rainey came. And I saw Galena then and I found it a fascinating town. Very beautiful area. But I loved all of it. I made great friends. I thought the university first rate. I had a delightful semester.

R G : Primarily teaching, was it?

P H : Yes. The one student I had who made an important name was Flannery O'Conner. But I hasten to add that I don't think I taught her much. She was already an artist and, really, an enigma . . . , and a painfully shy person, painfully. In our tutorials she would come and we would just stare at each other for an hour and a half—an occasional word. Not much. In her recent book of letters she says that she studied with me and paid me a compliment as a teacher. She said that I took a short story of hers and found forty things wrong with it. Well, I may have found one or two but I know it wasn't forty! Her letters are charming, by the way, and make a very nice book.

R G : So your "regionalism" (if it is such) is really East and West with very little Middle West?

P H : Not so much Middle West, no. Well, I've even written about California. Touched on San Francisco . . . in *Give Me Possession*. I consider myself a "transcontinental" American writer.

R G : It's a big canvas! What could you tell me about your experiences in New Mexico—all over New Mexico, north and south: Albuquerque, Santa Fe, Taos, Roswell, San Patricio, up and down the Rio Grande itself. That's a big list too.

P H : Well, *The Centuries of Santa Fe* is pretty clear—Santa Fe. *The Common Heart* deals with Albuquerque. *Far From Cibola* is straight Roswell. *The Thin Mountain Air* has [Magdalena] and Albuquerque. . . . *Whitewater* is Roswell put into West Texas. You know they call that quadrant of the state "Little Texas" because its indivisible from the Panhandle. A lot of aspects of Roswell got into *Whitewater*, as well as a lot of Texas.

R G : How about the Magdalena area?

P H : Yes, when I was a youngster I spent some time on a ranch in Magdalena, beyond Magdalena. I actually saw the sheep dipping process and it fascinated me always. (This is an example of the organic survival of thoughts.) Many years after that I wrote a short novel—in my Roswell days—dictated it actually. I thought I could do the story in all dialog. Sounded very natural. Dictated it. I had a good friend who was an excellent stenographer, and she could efface herself and I wasn't even aware of her as a medium. It was a short novel called "Sheep," and I turned it out in a certain number of days. It turned out to be about thirty-thousand words. Then I read it—I hadn't read it up to that point—and I threw it away! It was abominable! I could not dictate! The meaning of the word, the feel for the word, the texture of the word, the magic and the mystique of the word were absolutely missing! It was repetitive and banal and awful. But it dealt with the sheep dipping and I changed it greatly for *The Thin Mountain Air*.

R G : How about the patriarch and his wife in that novel? Real?

P H : Just in sketch form. They weren't realized, really. And their re-lationship wasn't as it was in the novel. But the central impulse and impetus of that event did not leave me and when it came, it came so naturally to be part of *The Thin Mountain Air* that I revisited those days in my imagination. And then the summer before I actually got into the novel I went back to the place—not the ranch itself, but the whole country, the landscape of Socorro and the highway west from Magdalena. Wonderful country! And it definitely was drawn from observation.

R G : That sort of "spot of time," the Wordsworthian "spot of time" technique which you are talking about, does that carry over as a kind of a process or a method where one salient memory will take over the whole book? Stimulate other things? Be the demarcation point.

P H : It certainly enters into it.

R G : Memories of your past, your childhood, seem a prominent part of all writing.

P H : Very organic. Of course, the obvious instance is Proust.

R G : Not so much [time in] Taos, you say?

P H : No, I facetiously have always felt, and have remarked, that you are either a Santa Fean or a Taosite. There's a kind of funny cultural rivalry between the places. And I like Santa Fe and I do not like Taos. I did not like Mrs. Luhan [Mabel Dodge] and all she stood for—all the social whim and aesthetic pretention I couldn't abide. I didn't like.

R G : When you go back to Santa Fe now, what do you do?

P H : Well I haven't been for several years. I have trouble with blood pressure there. The altitude is sort of too much for me. So, I haven't been back for, I suppose, four years.

R G : So it's more Albuquerque—when you return?

P H : No higher up than Albuquerque. More San Patricio, which is the same altitude as Albuquerque.

R G : As for the East—Rochester, Middletown, you love it here? This is home?

P H : Yes, very much so. As I said, the pattern of my life seems to be complete in coming back to the East without at all losing the Southwest. I still have to be there frequently. Aesthetically I love it. But this kind of life is very satisfying. There's one more area that I've written about in *Everything to Live For* which is the area around Chadds Ford and Wilmington, Delaware. That novel is the second in the Richard series. I refer to it as the DuPont barony—very rich. It's where Peter Hurd met his wife, Henriette Wyeth. I used to spend a great deal of time with them there. So that is the locale of *Everything to Live For*. And Dorchester, New York, is my convention for Buffalo and Rochester combined in the Richard novels—aspects of both cities I put together. When I needed an upstate New York setting it's always Dorchester.

RG: How about East-West journeys—westering. That's a theme in your novels.

PH: Well, it was a biographical accident that I became a westerner. When I was twelve we moved to Albuquerque. My father was tubercular. And that's what happened.

RG: Do you see parallels between you and Willa Cather as kinds of outcasts in the wilderness of the West? Pariahs out there? Did you feel "culture shock" even at that early age?

PH: I did, yes, moving to Albuquerque, even. I felt alien until the magic of the country overcame me and that took a year or two. But at first I was totally displaced. Well, I think any child would be, no matter where he would go. But then you know how the spell slowly overcomes you. So I think it was just a normal process. Then I was immensely seized by the scale and the grandeur and the beauty of the country—and the Rio Grande which I appropriated to my own imagination immediately almost. In fact, as much through Francis Fergusson as anything. Francis's grandfather was one of the great early founders of immigrant Albuquerque. And Francis was almost exactly my age and we grew up together, very closely. We were great friends. Erna's brother, Harvey's brother. And the whole Fergusson family were to me a great resource, and endless refreshment and enrichment. All so warm and charming. Civilized, deeply. So as soon as I got adjusted as a youth to the area, I was in an even more culturally advanced situation than I was in Buffalo. And Harvey was the first live author I'd ever met. I was thrilled to my boots to meet a real author.

R G : What is your thinking, both then and now, about the common western stereotypes, particularly of the Indian and the Mexican, and the changes that have taken place—evidenced in name changes such as Native American and Chicano . . . ?

P H : Nothing about it then, of course. I have a note about it in *The Thin Mountain Air* to adjust people who might think it either false or offensive, either way. That I refer to them as Mexicans. In fact many do become indignant if so called now. The stereotypes of course have always been there, and especially when one culture takes over another it immediately places an inferior status on the subject one. And gives it a stereotype. I think there is nothing more boring than a professional westerner. Or the professional Chicano. I hate very much the atomization of America which has happened. The national motto now means nothing: *e pluribus unum,* means nothing—out of many one, no longer. Now put it the other way: out of one many. Everybody is ethnically conscious and I think there is a big reflection throughout the country of this kind of breaking up. It's a subversive effect to culture in many ways. Everybody says it enriches everyone. The minute it gets self-conscious, then it gets commercial. That's the way America is. That's what I was saying about regionalism. The minute it is aware of itself . . . what makes it regional disappears. It becomes profitably functional. Self-consciously functional. And that I think is false, damaging, sad. It leads to the cliché of the so-called "western."

R G : Stegner . . . , you seem to have an affinity with Wallace Stegner here. He says this somewhere too.

P H : Yes, I like Stegner. And I think he's been a very good artist. . . .

R G : He talks about books and authors who traipse around in too much buckskin and wear their westernness too obviously.

P H : He's quite right. I'll never forget Oliver La Farge reviewing one of my books, I think it was *The Centuries of Sante Fe,* which on the whole he liked. And he said that Paul Horgan always dressed "eastern," implying that I never really became a New Mexican. Well, that's a piece of rubbish. I don't go around with a hat like rabbit's ears! And turquoise belts! People are at perfect liberty to do so if they want to. But it doesn't change anything, authentically. It seems to be so fatuous. People continuously go to the West now and reinvent the wheel. There's a new book out which just came the other day which I haven't read, but a friend of mine read it. It's about Taos and it's by the author of a novel called *The Sterile Cuckoo,* made into a movie.

R G : John Nichols; he also wrote *The Milagro Beanfield War.*

P H : Well, I haven't read him at all. But now he's talking about the *nativos* and the Spanish culture and Mexicans and the dispossesed and so on, as if no one else had ever noticed it. Of course he's an emigrant to Taos. Of course everybody repeats the same observation, the same thing. The pictures are abominable. It looks as if somebody has spilled catsup all over it. Like *Arizona Highways.* Hideous colorplates!

R G : What about the scenes in your books where an Indian is encountered—such as Dr. Rush in *The Common Heart.* What were your direct encounters with Indians?

P H : Mostly on the station platform at the Alvarado. When the trains came through they all got out their blankets and their wares. I don't remember it was an Indian. . . . Wasn't it a Mexican?

R G : In terms of the myth recounted, no, it's the Indian culture. Dr. Rush visits a pueblo too, remember, goes to the cliff dwellings later in the book?

PH: Oh yes, now I remember. I ran into an Indian on Gold Street who knew that I worked for the *Journal* and we fell into conversation about the "children of the Sun." Even then I didn't know if he was putting me on or not. But I didn't have any mystical experience, perhaps for the sake of the novel. But I always had a deep, fond feeling of respectful regard for the Pueblo establishment. The architecture. The concept of Pueblo life. The people that I knew. The dances. Erna [Fergusson] took me to my first one . . . and I was always very much moved by them. And so I had a great feeling, a very primitive feeling about the Indians. But I don't think I stereotyped them.

The Mexicans, when I first got there as a boy were treated as figures of fun, as cultural inferiors. Well, I'm afraid they were that by deprivation, not by nature. And yet when I wrote my biography of Lamy and saw that . . . and also read Gregg and other early reports of the Mexican in the nineteenth century in Santa Fe, there was a disposition of the Latin quite opposite of the Anglo-Saxon, which was regarded as inferior at the time, because it had different interests, different goals when judged by the Anglo-Saxon standard, by which they fell very short in terms of energy, in terms of getting there, in terms of drive—our type . . . , my type of standard. So I suppose at the time I didn't have the sensitivity which I later developed about the real quality of the Spanish inheritance.

RG: Did you have any conscious admiration or any special notions about the concepts of time in your portrayals of Indians and Mexican Americans?

PH: No. I never even thought about it.

RG: One critic goes to great lengths to explain how you valued Indian and Mexican concepts of time in your writings.

PH: Mine? Gracious. It's like having, you know, whatever you write somebody will put a symbol in it. There's a hilarious story about Mary McCarthy going back to Vassar where she once taught. A year later she went back and met former students and asked one of them how she was getting along. And the girl said, "Oh just fine, Professor Soandso really likes one of my stories." "Is it finished?" asked McCarthy. "Oh, yes it's finished," came the reply, " . . . but next Tuesday we're going to put in the symbols!"

That's an experience imposed from without all the time. Anything that's true can be a symbol. And whether its conscious or not, or whether it's part of the scheme or not, half the time, nine-tenths of the time the author doesn't mean, . . . I don't think Melville meant all the stuff that's attributed to him . . . and the whale, the mystique, and symbols, any of it other than he was writing a roaring good yarn. Well, that's wrong; I take it back. I don't mean to be disrespectful. It's a significant and an important work. It's a work of art. But I don't think it has to have all this aura about it, which many an academic career has been based on.

RG: Now I'd like to turn to questions about Catholicism. Is it true that Oliver La Farge once criticized you for overplaying Catholicism in your writing?

PH: I think he did. I forget in what connection . . . but I think it was *Great River.* His review of that was in the *New York Times* and also in the *Santa Fe New Mexican.* He reviewed it twice. Yes, it was Oliver who thought that I leaned a little heavily on the words as well as the presence of the Catholic.

RG: Do you see books like *Rome Eternal* as being significant to your overall body of work?

PH: Oh, that's not very significant. Obviously its chief interest to me was aesthetic. I have no question about the need and structure and inherent content of the Church. I was interested in providing word images for the film. Have you seen that film? It played, I think, three or four times on national television. You'll see that although the religious theme is a constant it still leans more toward the historical and the aesthetical.

RG: If you were characterized as a Catholic writer what would be your response?

PH: I have been many times and my response has been to reverse it—a writer who is a Catholic. Graham Greene said the same thing. It's an obvious thing. Catholicism is indivisible, what I see and what I do, but it isn't a mission I'm on as an apostolic.

RG: Sometimes you're a little harsh on it, aren't you?

PH: Yes, on aspects of it. Harsher now than before on the changes. But they have not come into my world. My Catholicism has to be recognized, and it has to be seen as a vital strand of my total capacity. Don't you think? It was an inheritance. It's one that grows stronger with knowledge rather than just acceptance. I think it's the absolute backbone of western civilization and that insofar as one attaches oneself to that tradition, I think it's inescapably powerful and significant. It's like a second skin, really. I don't even think about it. Where would most of the art in all media be if it weren't for the impulse of the Church?

RG: It was a pretty strong influence in your youth, then. You say it was inherited?

PH: Yes. Yes, on both sides, father and mother. I think man has always looked for one single explanation to account for everything, good or bad, evil, life or death, and so on. The affirmative or the negative. And it has always seemed to me that the Church, Catholicism, is that answer.

RG: You haven't said, "I'm going to deliberately incorporate this in what I write"?

PH: No, it's just been one of the strands of my experience. One draws on it quite automatically and almost unthinkingly.

R G : Along with Catholicism, your experiences in the military seem to be part of that biographical braiding. You wrote a "best-seller" while in the army? The booklet for the troops on venereal disease?

P H : Yes, it had a first printing of two or three million copies! I've passed two million with one or two of my own works—*Whitewater* went over two million in all editions and probably *A Distant Trumpet* went over two and a half million. But that book was commissioned by the Surgeon General and I was chief of the Army Information Branch in Washington at the Pentagon, which provided information for the troops, not the public, through every conceivable means of communication: film, radio, recording, graphics—all kinds of ways. The rate of venereal disease was terrifying. And I tried to think, "To whom on our staff can I throw this job?" Well, I kept seeing it in terms of very simple drawings, very simple text, very punchy message—as if I were an advertising man—and I decided to do it myself. And I did, and Gen. Will Menninger, the great psychiatrist, and head of this division in the Surgeon General's office, approved it and it went to press. Well, to my amazement I had a call from General Menninger not long afterward, saying that the VD rate had dropped dramatically.

R G : What exactly were your duties during the war years?

P H : Well, they were very complicated. There was a thing called the Information and Education Division, and my branch, of which I became chief, was charged with informing the troops about various matters—news, the life at home, and soldiering. The whole division had about four or five branches. The Information Branch was largest and the most far-reaching. The next was the Education Branch which gave troops the opportunity to study, all over the world, to earn, in fact credit. Then there was an Orientation Branch, a Research Branch, and the like.

The Information Division published *Yank,* the army weekly, twenty-six editions around the world every week. And all the army news service transmission—over a hundred thousand words a day to soldier papers everywhere throughout the world. And the "Why We Fight" films made by Colonel Frank Capra, the director. And the booklets for recruits going to foreign countries. Neat little War Department booklets. Brilliantly written, mostly. And an army/navy screen magazine. Recordings, the armed forces radio service—all this came under me. For about three and a half years we were one of the biggest publishers in the world. Just as it happened. It was a very sympathetic job and I was lucky to be assigned to it. I wasn't originally appointed chief of the branch. After my boss became a general I was given his job. It was a fascinating undertaking, headquarters in the Pentagon but with some offices all over the world, in every theater of war. It was information to troops. It was enormously absorbing. And somewhat wearing I guess. I didn't have a day's leave in four years. I worked constantly. There's another story in *The Peachstone,* by the way, called "Old Army," which deals with those years.

RG: Do you have any ambivalence at all toward soldiering?

PH: No, I've always felt at home with the military and in the military. First of all through the school [New Mexico Military Institute]. I was an officer and held rank—which everyone did by order of the governor of New Mexico. But I made a transition into army rank without difficulty. And found myself, really, aside from two or three regular officers, the only one with any military background. So I was perfectly at ease. My first assignment was to go to Hollywood and make a film with Capra's outfit on the officer candidate system. And aside from the young lieutenant who was the adjutant who had been through OCS, I was the only one who knew what military life was, what drill was, so I found myself drilling these Hollywood experts and technicians, people who came into uniform from enormous positions in the film colony. I put them through calesthenics in the morning and platoon drill. It was killingly funny to see them try to conform. It was quite unnecessary. But it was part of it.

When I finally was given command of the branch in Washington, my staff—all my office, commissioned and noncommissioned, were known as "Horgan's Dudes" in the War Department because I made them polish their brass. But it seemed to me important that we show well. No, I have a great feeling for the service. Snow makes an interesting point in his essay about my feeling for the army in a time when it was not fashionable to feel sympathetic for it. But some of the most imaginative people I've ever known were the people I served with in the army. I have great respect for them. My first boss was almost a genius in terms of imaginative concepts. He was a West Pointer named E. L. Munson.

R G : Let me turn again for a minute to music and painting and literature and how you see the interrelationships. You know quite a bit about all these fields.

P H : The applications? Well, I think the musical faculty expresses itself first of all and most importantly in a feeling for form—that is, you know, of strictly formal . . . as an abstract thing music is. That is of inestimable analogous value, it seems to me, for the serious writer. It also plays a great part in an ear for rhythm. And I think the key to readability in prose is rhythm. That seems to me to be a very direct value, that one trains oneself by listening, through listening—not consciously trains but acquires through listening or through performing—any relation to music in more than a desultory way. So, it isn't that one wants to write a novel like a symphony. That's a sophomoric idea. Every young writer wants to create a work in four movements, like a symphony. Well, that's nonsense. That isn't what I mean by analogous form at all. What is meant is a sense of design. Theme developing into something having a consequence. And from the consequence coming a logical jump to a conclusion. Just a resolution, you see, finally of the three given elements. But so many writers don't have any sense of this. They just proceed and its over. Or they arbitrarily have things happen and its over.

R G : So it's the kind of thing E. M. Forster talks about in *Aspects of the Novel* in the chapter on "Pattern and Rhythm." A writer needs a sense of the internal and external stitching?

P H : Right. Yes, right. But this also must be true and be internally motivated by the characters. So it plays back and forth. Now as to painting, every novelist, every writer of fiction must have a strong visual sense, must have a pictorial knack and a differentiation between matters of volume and composition and color and perspective even, and all the details that make up a scene. They've got to be S-E-E-N! And if you draw, you try very hard as you're drawing to catch what you're looking at. Well, then it becomes a similar process when you try to bring that into words. I think drawing and painting are very direct contributors to writing.

* * *

R G : Do you have any special approach to biography which you follow or which you prefer?

P H : I don't think a psychological, systematic concept is the key. I'm not a Freudian. I don't believe in those principles of Freud. They're very limited, derived from his imaginative experience by a certainly brilliant man. Debatably but perhaps with therapeutic value, but they do not translate into literary value for me. In a certain way, it's analogous to having a fixed concept of a view of life before starting to analyze anything. For instance, if I were an economist or a social historian, everything would have to conform to Marxism, if I were writing from that stance. Well, I wouldn't be, because I'm very much anti-Marx and his view. . . .

So in terms of writing biography I think, again, the intuition of the artist is much more important than any fixed theory of how to treat a character. The strict facts and the strict information will give you keys to that intuition for biographical purpose, I think. For example, I didn't make up anything about Lamy. But everything I read about Lamy gave me a consistent view of him. Miss Cather's book about him is, of course, a novel and she had every right to improvise and she did. She invented much more than was factually true. And it's odd that in many reviews of my book it's been compared to her novel in terms of actual fact, which is irrelevant to her book. She had a fine sense of his character, his nature. It's a beautifully written work but it is not biography. And it's very hard for some reviewers to separate the two.

R G : Well, that's an inevitable comparison. Any time your book comes up people naturally go back to hers.

P H : Yes, yes. But the values involved are quite different.

R G : How about your approaches to history? Any notions there?

P H : I think I'd have to recapitulate what I just said about biography but add that history as literature is a very reachable and a very important goal, provided that there is some literary gift involved. But again, the instrument of prose, of good prose, can be as able a servant of truth as mere factuality and therefore that which interests me is always that which is best written.

R G : I'm fascinated by the title of one of your novels [*Memories of the Future*] because I see echoes of that paradoxical theme in your other work.

P H : That's a sweet title, isn't it? The novel is about World War II and a family in the war—based on a family I knew. They were chief members of the cast, stationed in Mexico City as a naval attaché, and his wife and child. And in Mexico City there was a little café called Recuerdos del Porvenir and it translated "memories of the future," and they always laughed about that and loved the idea. Finally it turned out that at one time there was a café called "El Porvenir," the future. But it burned down and when it was rebuilt they called it Recuerdos del Porvenir, "memories of the future." In the novel this comes up as part of the experience of that family. And when the tragedy in the family occurs they try to recover from it; one of the characters says, in effect, "Well, aren't all our lives built on memories of the future?" The theme, as I see it, is only peculiar to that novel.

RG: How about the theme of maturation, of loss of innocence, in your novels? That's pervasive.

PH: That's certainly the theme of the Richard novels. I wouldn't think it's a major theme of any of the others. Certainly the strongest impressions one gets are prepubescent. And they constantly come back in vividness and one imagines the consequences of these first impressions. And therefore they're powerful, powerful motivations toward writing. But I don't really see it as a major motivation in my own books. In the case of the Richard novels, only the first one deals with the preadolescent years. That's Richard from about four to twelve or a little after. The next one is the adolescent, mid or late adolescent, late prep school. And the third one is the collegiate years. One thing no critic has picked up, which interests me, about these three books, is the difference in tone. The first is written in a tone which is appropriate to very young experience. Like a glass of water, clear and simple. The next one has some of the romantic and lyric confusions of that time of life in the very prose, the very instrument. The third is the beginning of the adult and has the complications that come with the farther discoveries. And that I think is in the prose—very much more sober kind of writing than in the first one. Or the second one. Perhaps even more sophisticated. But it was a device, a deliberate approach to these three things, three phases, and as such seems inseparable from an understanding of these three books. But none of them noticed.

RG: And the next one would have been much older in tone?

PH: That would have been much later in life and had a much different tone.

RG: How do you see those books, the Richard trilogy, relative to your other novels?

PH: It would be pointless to classify them, each with a different concept to realize. Nothing schematic about them. The sequence, the succession. And no favorites, actually. I think some novels do some things better than othes. For instance, I think in terms of the achievement of form, in both an original and an appropriate way, the most successful is *Far From Cibola*. It was the thing I've never done before or since. But other novels have penetrated otherwise, have taken different shapes for different reasons. In its way I'm very fond of *No Quarter Given*, which is long, huge, a terribly long book. I reread it recently and it seems to me a good novel, of which one of the English critics said, "A moment of greatness." I'll accept that. And I'd like to see it back in print. But it's so enormously long and would be so expensive to restore. The concept is that all the auto-biographical sections are analogies for his music—the music which flows from his life. Rather than put down descriptions of his symphonies, actual compositions, the substance is presented. So every now and then the narrative of the present in Santa Fe breaks into Edmund's past and its phases.

R G : A fine design and a really good book!

P H : If I may say so without bumptiousness, I think it's an important novel. And among mine I think it's among the half-dozen best. It's a picture of a certain cultural vein through Edmund's experience which I don't think has ever been put down in fiction. The New York theater and musical world—all that. The early movie palace world. I don't know anything else that's gotten that.

R G : No chance for a reissue?

P H : I've asked Farrar Straus about it and the feeling is that since it would be a reissue it wouldn't get reviewed and therefore it wouldn't get sold. It was published in 1935, long before paperback editions.

R G : How about your way with endings? I've always been struck by how you round off a chapter.

P H : Resolutions? Again, that's musical. They can be given elements of a passage or a work or any part of it. That must have design and it must not be left hanging unless there's a vital reason to pick it up later. In general what you call endings are technically quite necessary for the artistic unit, whether it be a cell in a whole series or whether it be the whole work. I often don't think of it. It just seems to me as I reach a certain phase of the narrative that that's the thing which should be done to it. Frank Capra while I was working with him—he's become one of my life-long friends—was talking about the movie script I wrote for the army. . . . I was inexperienced, and there is a craft of script writing and I have great respect for it. One reason I did not take a Hollywood job is that I thought I would have to take a long apprenticeship, much too long, successfully to deal with the film medium. In other words I wasn't about to go slumming and pick up a lot of money as a lot of people did. But Capra said one day in a meeting with me that my script was this and my script was that but among other things that it lacked was this very thing. The sense of ending. He said, "You must always at the end of every scene, Paul, . . . there has to be a *topper.*" Now that is a film maker's recipe. And if you do take theater and film you will see that it's part of show biz to end on one higher note. One conclusive thrust of some kind. So I tried to work that into what I was doing for Capra. But it wasn't a conscious decision of mine in terms of that kind of show biz thing—in its way a kind of aesthetic—but to me it came from another source. The sense of resolution. I hadn't conceived it. Let's put it that way.

RG: Some people talk of closed endings and expansive endings. I've always thought of your endings, chapter endings, especially, as expansive.

PH: You mean in the sense that the meaning lingers afterwards? Well, that's what I hope for. Very much so. You know it's said to be behind Chinese poetry. That the poem begins when the words end. I got this from Bynner who was a great translator of Chinese poetry. Probably the greatest. And he once enunciated this to me. The function of the Chinese poem is to arouse. Whatever the content of the poem was, when the words end you carry on with it.

RG: What about your treatment of violence in your novels?

PH: When violence is a consequence of character, as in *The Thin Mountain Air,* you deal with it. For its own gratuitous sake it is meaningless artistically. That's what is wrong with so much of the pop media, television, pop books and such. There's not much more to say about it, except that it's often mindless and arbitrary, idiotic, wrong, awful. But it can be and often is a direct outgrowth of human nature and in that case if you are dealing with a certain kind of human nature, it must have its expression.

RG: What are your attitudes toward sexuality in your fiction?

PH: Well, as for sex, I would say pretty much the same thing. It is an extension of a natural being or it is an unnatural imposition and therefore not of artistic or of literary value. I think in today's social terms which have very little to do with what I write, that it's greatly, . . . , well, it's too pop. I'll put it that way. The privacy of the sexual relationship has been so invaded, so opened out in group interest,— it seems to be irrelevant to its nature. Private sex is another matter. And should be left so.

RG: And your views about feminism, issues of how a male author might treat women in fiction?

PH: Again, I think the feminine strain in any artist has a chance for its expression in the depiction of women, either in painted portraiture or word development or whatever. They say that no man can write well about a woman. I don't think that's true. I think Tolstoy did. Many did. Flaubert did. I think Maurice Baring did, wonderfully. So I don't see any significant difference really. The novel I'm currently working on has the central character of a woman. I feel that she's there, that she's alive, that how she responds is true to that particular woman. I won't say that she's a monument to womanhood. That isn't my purpose.

RG: Well, I do feel that your women characters are convincing. There are many different kinds of women readers and even feminist readers. So "convincing" becomes relative.

PH: You try to see women as individuals and if you do, then their idiosyncracies and realities are to be recognized and captured, that's all, as one does with a man character. I don't see any reason to separate these.

RG: Why haven't you written more books like *Toby and the Nighttime*, books for young readers?

PH: I have. The very first book I published was called *Men at Arms*, which was a picture book. Only five hundred copies were bound. And then Farrar Straus asked me to do a juvenile and I did, *Toby*. And that's all. The only reason I wrote it is because they asked me to. And I don't feel a natural affinity for it, much as I love children and their devastating honesty.

RG: What about eloquence and simplicity, the choice of the right word in writing?

PH: It's a part of style, of the instrument, a part of a love for the language. And a feeling for finding, if not really achieving, the perfectly clear but nonhackneyed expression. The trouble with clichés is that they say what they mean but they get very tiresome. I certainly began early in life, after my first imitative flings, to erase efforts at being grand in style. And the closer I've come to simplicity, the better I think I've managed. But that does not foreclose eloquence. Or originality, sometimes to the point of being arresting. I think there is a great deal in *Great River* which is rather dense and rich writing. But the subject matter seemed to me to require it absolutely. The scene and the thunder of some of the episodes and some of the events.

RG: So you don't see a split between form and content? Style is not a condiment.

PH: Oh, no, no, no. You don't sprinkle it in, put it in afterward like symbols.

RG: But in some of your earliest [unpublished] novels like *The Golden Rose* style is too prominent?

PH: Yes, that obviously was very precious, very precious. And I would erase that.

RG: How about contemporary novel theory . . . ? Are you much concerned with that?

PH: No. I don't know anything about it. Much of it is approached from two points of view. One is the Freudian and its offshoots; and the other is Marxist and its modifications. And neither of them interests me at all. Neither of them seems relevant to a literary performance. Unless it is propagandistic or persuasive deliberately. Then it's probably useful. But to me not interesting. As for modern criticism, I've been very much outside the mode. You'll find it in *Approaches to Writing*, and it's a natural attitude and one I've cultivated.

RG: John Gardner's recent book *On Moral Fiction* presents some views which I see as similar to yours.

PH: Really. I think that in terms of serious criticism and serious recognition, serious position, I don't seem to have it. If I had been more modish I would have had more prominence in "intellectual" circles; but what that's based on doesn't interest me.

RG: In terms of publishing and agents, you seem to have had a great relationship with Virginia Rice.

PH: Oh yes, Virginia was my agent for many years. I was still a sprout in Rochester and knew a dear friend of hers there, Lulu Wile. . . . They went to Wellesley together. And after I moved West, Virginia set up in business as an agent. She wrote randomly to Lulu and said, "Where can I get some writers?" and Lulu said get PH. So Virginia wrote to me and from that came this relationship. She was infinitely loyal and indefatigable and had a very small list. She would not have any assistants because she didn't want anyone else to handle her people. And finally, toward the end of her life, I was her only client. She was a major general at the job and a dear friend up until the end and her illness.

R G : And you have a good relationship with your present publisher?

P H : Oh yes, Robert Giroux and Roger Straus. And that came about through Virginia. I was with Harper and then after I came out of the army I couldn't stay because my editor there, Eugene Saxton, died. He was magnificent. With Max Perkins he was the other great editor of his era. And I was then committed to finish *Great River* for Rinehart and I had no other book to go ahead with, except *Memories of the Future* (which I wrote in Iowa City, by the way, in four months). There was no need for an immediate publishing connection because *Great River* had to be finished. And finally that was delivered to Rinehart. Then Virginia began thinking and finally she thought she'd bring Giroux and me together. He was then with Harcourt Brace. We took to each other right away. Had an immediate understanding of writing—much the same way. So he asked me to sign up with Harcourt and I did, and they honored me with an immediate advance. And about eight or ten months into this contract he broke with them and wrote to me and said "I'm leaving, will you go with me to Farrar Straus?" And I said, "Certainly, but can I get free?" Well, in effect they bought me out. I gave the advance back to Harcourt. Luckily I had not yet given them a book. And Giroux took away myself and T. S. Eliot and Father Merton, Jean Stafford, and I can't tell you who else.

* * * *

R G : Two questions: What kind of fan mail do you get and do you have any regrets about what you could have written and didn't?

PH: Well, let me say a bit about my correspondence. I get a few, few, letters addressed "Dear F-R-E-I-N-D"—worthy but illiterate responses. I suppose everyone does. Mostly the letters about my work come late, come considerably after publication. I'd say that I have a fair number of habitually and probably friendly readers who really get what I do, and mean to do.

RG: About the regrets question . . . ?

PH: Oh, the regrets question. Well, . . . sometimes I'm sorry I wasn't Toscanini. If I'm reincarnated I'd like to be a conductor because I think it's a tremendous expression. Though perhaps I should have preferred to have been Beethoven because it's creative. In literary terms, I never have been fully satisfied with the performance, with the complete public work. It's always beyond grasp.

RG: You could go back and revise everything endlessly?

PH: Oh, no I couldn't do that. No, I couldn't do that. First, I don't think it's honest; and, secondly, once the vision, to whatever degree it's been grasped, or captured, or seen, or fulfilled, there's nothing more to do about it. Even stylistically. I thought once of revising *No Quarter Given* in terms of style because it's very full of young extravagances, but they belong in some curious way. So I don't think I could do that. If I've erred in terms of fact, in any of my historical and biographical facts, I would like to correct that.

In fact, in *Great River* I've made two general revisions. And the third edition, the paperback which is now in print, which so far as I could make it is the correct one, the corrected one. But regrets are very hard to pin down. It's very hard to turn back. I don't mean to sound self-satisfied.

RG: What would be a crucially important question to ask Paul Horgan about his writing? One key question you might ask yourself?

P H : About the writings? You limit it to that? It's a terrible question . . . , "What would I ask myself? A key question about my writing?" I'm trying to pin down what I would ask myself, I take it about performance or satisfaction?

R G : Not necessarily. . . . Something about understanding, about getting at the essential Paul Horgan? Perhaps taste? Sensibilities?

P H : I suppose I could summarize something like this: that believing as I do in the function of the writer as embracing more than one kind of writing, one kind of form, one kind of medium—that is, fiction or nonfiction, history or . . . whatever—that in my writing at least I've attempted the appropriate response to the appropriate form, the appropriate meaning, and that's been a conscious process.

That is, I haven't written fiction like history or history like fiction. I've sometimes composed attributes of the two or parts of the craft, so they've been overlapped. It just seems to me that provided truth is respected, there is nothing wrong with *using* the craft of the novelist in history in creating the scene—I want the reader at the scene. But not to betray the truth in any sense as I've been able to discover it. So it comes back again to the question, "Do I think in all the variety of my work there has been a fairly consistent attitude?" I would say yes, given the necessity for versatility among the various forms with which I've dealt. So there's a kind of unity, I think, in what I've done, no matter what its variety suggests.

R G : Do you see that same kind of unity to your life?

P H : Well, the life has had phases, but I think throughout there has been a consistent thread. And I think that is probably a combination of, for want of a better than current word, a certain respect for humanism as an attitude, not a system, and the religious vein we've already touched on, and a kind of aesthetic fastidiousness, I guess—a sense of choice between the excellent and the good, the beautiful and the adequate, and so on.

All right, put it down in another very unpopular word—elite. I like the idea of an elite, provided it has been earned, not bestowed. An elite implies a choice of values, and that I've tried to make in favor of the superior, the true, the just and (to sound Victorian), the beautiful.

The Enduring Values
of Paul Horgan: Interview

RG : First let me ask about your three most recent books—*A Certain Climate, A Writer's Eye,* and *Under the Sangre de Cristo.* As usual, they are fine testimonials to the art of bookmaking above and beyond the art of authorship. You see the physical form and function of a book as significant, and address this in your essay "The Climate of Books." Could you comment here a bit more on the book as object or process?

PH : I have always been devoted to the art of typography and book design. When I take up a new book the first thing I do is lift away the jacket and examine the binding; and then I open to the title page, and I follow this with an examination of the page designs in the rest of the book to see whether the book as a whole has had a consistent design. If the book has been designed with style appropriate to its contents, and if it reflects a high degree of style and taste in its physical embodiment, my enjoyment of the text is heightened. In the matter of my own books, I have been lucky to have publishers who indulged my ideas about design. General book design in this country took a turn for the better when Alfred A. Knopf began publishing on his own before 1920. He created fine new possibilities with typography and binding materials; and he led the publishing world into a new era of expression. Dreary routines continue to dominate many manufacturers of books; but many of the leading houses now retain excellent designers, to my personal pleasure.

R G : You obviously agree with Carlyle that "a good book is the purest essence of the soul." What's behind a sentiment like that? Do you think it is consciously held by most writers and readers?

P H : I would qualify Carlyle's "purest essence" by suggesting that it is music which best deserves this description. Yet a most satisfying relation, in utmost privacy, is set up between the reader, the book, and its invisible author.

R G : As one of the few true men of letters in contemporary American literature, you've expressed your feelings and ideas in a number of literary forms, fiction and nonfiction. Is the essay still as viable as a form as it was in the eighteenth century? Do you tend to integrate or separate the various modes of discourse or literary forms?

P H : It has always seemed to me that to be a writer implies opportunity in all literary forms. For myself, I will say that it is the subject matter that determines the form—novel, story, essay, history, biography, criticism, memoir—which will best serve it. The essay seems useful not only to me, but to a fairly plentiful roster of other writers, judging by the number of essay collections that continue to show up on publishers' lists. As for the integration of modes of discourse—perhaps a most interesting form of this can be seen in certain uses of the documentary film, in which essayistic commentary accompanies visual projections.

R G : What about the boundaries between history and biography, or history, biography, and fiction? It seems true but also paradoxical that artists, maybe novelists, as you suggest, make the best writers of history. That's a rather controversial point in historiography these days, isn't it?—the social scientist, the quantifier, and the statistician, drawing the line in the dust and saying, "Better not to cross it" to the writer of fiction. I exaggerate, but what is involved in the issue of history and narrative as you see it?

P H : There are of course many phases of history, biography, and even techniques of fiction, which cloud over each other. Separation of these is difficult. History, the chronicle of past times, cannot be told except through the events of human life. Biography cannot be richly set forth unless the backgrounds and social atmosphere of the subject are evoked. The forward impulsion of a chronicle can often be beautifully served by the instrument of narrative as used by a competent novelist. Further, the resources of the literary artist—sense of form, eye for detail, mastery of proportion, intuition of human nature, delight in environment, and above all a gift for breathing life into character—can properly be brought into the writing of history provided that historical truth, so far as the historian can determine it, is not violated. All works of historiography are subject to later revision as hitherto unavailable facts are unearthed. Honorably used in the service of historical truth, the devices of the literary artist provide the one constant in a work of history or biography in its time, until inevitably overtaken by revelations of continuing research. The "social scientist, the quantifier, and the statistician" bring their technical observations; the literary artist brings his values; neither need exclude the other—indeed, cannot do so, if the gifts of each are unified in the person of the historian himself. It is such completeness we hope for, no matter how rarely we find it.

R G : The questions of the boundaries of genre and mode are matched currently with issues about relationships between the regional and the universal in literature. You never have thought of yourself as a regionalist, certainly not a western writer, have you? Does it make a difference how writers classify themselves or how readers tend to classify them?

P H : The whole issue is simply a celebration of locality. Worthy and worthless books are written about any geographical or social background. To elevate the concept of regionalism into a whole philosophy of genre seems to me naive, and to classify writers accordingly seems ultimately to be of less consequence than their evaluation as literary artists. There have been beautiful works of fiction written about cowboys, sheriffs, ranchers and their world, along with mountains of innocently profitable trash. All too often their common subject matter unites both levels of value in a genre that an indiscriminate public, and many critics, heap together. Works of history, biography, natural history, social subjects, related by the geography of the American West, come under a different set of values. Here is actually the locale that is the central consideration; and here a classification according to "region" seems not only just but inevitable, and the old label "western" falls out of sight, and evaluation of such works is made with a proper regard for their thematic background. As for classification by or of writers—the question comes shamelessly down to a matter of book sales, and the reading public's taste, educational level, and powers of recognition.

R G : Ellen Goodman and others have recently talked about the "dumbing down" of American mind and taste. Do you see that?

P H : The immense pervasiveness of pop media of information—TV, movies, junk journalism, and, subliminally, rock music—has certainly lowered the general quotient of the current mentality; and so has the woefully indifferent system of general public education, all the way up the lifeline from primary grades, through high school, and into college curricula. Dreadful dilemmas do face those in charge of the educational apparatus at large. Costs of every sort rise fast. Casual life patterns result in slackness of manners and morals. The breakdown of family stability (fifty percent divorce rate) leads to the loss of disciplinary habits and parental examples of respectability. Low pay forces good teachers out of the classroom and attracts as recruits many who are unqualified. The public climate of mind is steadily and disastrously debased by moronic TV and movie images of life and behavior that positively incite the young to imitation. The result is an anti-ethic of violence, drug acceptance, and sexual irresponsibility certain to erode the whole society's self-preserving values of decency and judgment. "Dumbing down" is wildly profitable to purveyors of entertainment and advertising. Popular education is largely in their hands. God save the Republic, as Mr. Mencken used to say.

R G : Such as the 1988 presidential campaign spectacle?

P H : In the 1988 presidential campaign there was no evidence of an encompassing vision of the nation and its still empowering heritage, its needs, its future direction. The nominees were lost in expedient exploitations of the lesser specifics, which they championed in an unworthy exchange of foul personal accusations. In his extravagant praise of his running mate, Vice President Bush was either a naif or a cynic—neither an acceptable character for the presidency. Governor Dukakis' manner of delivery—a fast-talking little tough guy tumbling out his self-recommendations—denied his ideas their chance to be understood. Yet how strange: when read in transcript, the governor's statements were lucid, sensible if not inspiring. Those of the vice president were like whining protests of virtue misconstrued. Both parties were denied decent reality because of their manipulation by their backstage handlers. Dubious "show-biz" values and cheap ideas of "strategy" destroyed perception of whatever personal truth and decent worthiness each candidate possessed. For the voter it was a frustrating exhibition all the way, and it was brought about through the apparent actuality of a picture taken on the spot, a picture in living color, a picture that could talk, a picture that could be edited to an often dubious purpose. The voter, whatever his alliance, was left with an apathetic disappointment, tinged with a smouldering sense that he, and the nation, in its travail, deserved far better in honor of the presidency itself. Many felt that a debasement of the national self-image had occurred.

R G : Your point in *A Writer's Eye* about needing to draw or paint your records of some of your travels and field research for *Great River, Lamy of Santa Fe,* and *Conquistadors in North American History,* and the inadequacy of a camera for such purposes leads me to wonder about your views on technology generally.

P H : Drawing and painting are, for me, more directly personal and intimate than making a photograph. The feeling involved is more direct; and it is the feeling about what I draw that I hope to recapture later, using my little pictures as reminders. In general, the fewer the interventions by gadgets between myself and my text, the greater the control that I hold over it. The computer seems to me more elaborate than a typewriter. Moreover, with pen I rework my typed text over and over, at different times. If I understand it properly, the famous virtue of revision by word processor can be done only at a single time, while the text is on the screen. I want more than one chance to improve my draft. Technology has its wonders— and its perils. The mere concept, let alone enactment, of "artificial intelligence" scares the hell out of me.

RG: You've enjoyed the friendship and company of some interesting and eminent individuals in your life. But as you offer your portraitures of Henriette Wyeth (or Peter Hurd), or Alice Roosevelt Longworth or Rouben Mamoulian, they seem almost on the same level of knowledgeability for the reader as do Willa Cather or Jean Baptiste Lamy or other historical personages who have been subjects for your biographies. How do you account for such verisimilitude in your work as biographer?

PH: If I have brought my biographical subjects and fictional characters alive to the degree you suggest, I am grateful. I suppose I try to know as much as I can about my subjects and then through a mélange of the facts, I enter into a state of feeling about them, and then with my two avenues of perception, I try to translate the perception into words.

RG: How much influence did your chance encounter with Cather, in the La Fonda Hotel in Santa Fe when you were a youth, have on your historical pursuit of of Lamy? Was Cather really at work on *Death Comes for the Archbishop* when you intruded so surprisingly and unavoiadably on her? Was that an instance of fate working out life's little ironies?

PH: Poor Miss Cather. I interrupted her work—quite unaware that she was at work on the La Fonda balcony where I went to get a view up the street. I retreated instantly when I saw her and her companion-secretary. I knew what it meant to have your concentration interrupted while at work. I assume she was working on Lamy, but I can't say for certain. My awkward encounter had nothing to do with my own efforts years later to write my Lamy book.

R G : I can't help asking you a bit more about your D. H. Lawrence story, "So Little Freedom" which appears again in *Under the Sangre de Cristo*. You seem to satirize just about everyone involved, the aspiring boy artist, the Mabel Dodge Luhan figure, and certainly David Herbert Lawrence. Your description of his western dress and demeanor, in all its glorious satire, is reflected too in your delightfully funny clerihews. I know you and Witter Bynner were friends, but did you know the Taos crowd in the 1920s—Mrs. Luhan, Tony? You chose not to settle in the artists' colonies of Taos and Santa Fe. And La Farge commented on your eastern flair as a cause. Why didn't you settle in Santa Fe?

P H : Lawrence was dead when I reappeared on the New Mexican scene in the twenties. I did meet and become very fond of Frieda Lawrence. I met Mrs. Luhan once only, without becoming fond. Those aspects of both Taos and Santa Fe that assume the character of "artists' colonies" appealed to me only in my extreme youth. Those seemed most intense and noticeable in Taos, possibly because Taos is much smaller than Santa Fe, and because Santa Fe is characterized by a more sophisticated general level of life. I visited Santa Fe often, lived there for a few months at a time, knew enriching friendships, and deeply loved the superb country all about. I miss my intermittent life there.

R G : Insofar as you are a writer East and West and have known both worlds, both ambiences, why did you prefer to move back to an eastern residence and remain there after so many years living in New Mexico?

P H : While living in Santa Fe in 1962 I was appointed director of the

Center for Advanced Studies at Wesleyan University, and forthwith moved to Middletown, Connecticut. It was an appointment that greatly interested me, and my years in that position brought me a wonderfully stimulating life in the world of ideas and creative work in the company of the fellows of the center, for whose appointment and subsequent university residence I was responsible. They were a remarkable company of men and women, representing high achievement in the arts, science, government, religion, philosophy. To be their presiding associate was both an honor and a super-education; and the job permitted me to get on with my own writing—indeed, to be actively at work in my own fields seemed appropriate to my administrative task of fostering the ongoing work of the fellows in residence. At the end of my five-year directorship, the university allowed me to remain as adjunct professor and author in residence. For some time I made annual and semiannual trips to New Mexico, but in time these had to be given up for reasons related to advancing age and attendant inconveniences of unreliable health. It was no hardship for me to resume life in the East. I was born in New York state. New England had many beautiful aspects of land and climate in common with my earliest environment. In my years of life out West I constantly traveled eastward for professional, and cultural, contacts, and for friendships. I found no hardship at either end of our continent.

RG: Your essays, your writing, and your life indicate that style is of crucial importance to you. How would you define it, and why is it so important? What is your style as a writer?—an important question in light of some critics thinking that your style is at times overly mannered and self-conscious, and other critics believing that you are a writer's writer, a stylistic virtuoso.

PH: Oh, style is simply one's signature. Its perception by others surely must depend on their capacity to appreciate it. In any case, I mustn't complain when I am accused of literacy.

RG: Some might infer that, given all the time you spend writing and reading, you are something of an indoor person, not given to getting out in nature. And yet nature and outdoor settings are done so successfully in your books, and even your travels up and down the Rio Grande dispel any such mistaken notions of your estrangement from nature. In any sense do you consider yourself a nature writer, even a writer with a kind of ecological conscience or message (as opposed to a drawing-room conscience or message, I guess)?

PH: . . . No, I am not a "nature" writer, nor have I any message about the environment as such. . . . I would patiently add that the ecology of the drawing room is quite as valid in the way of literary material as any other environment in which human beings find themselves.

RG: Do you really think the book will bear against barbarism and see civilization through, as you suggest in your "Allegory" which ends *Climate*? What's the climate for such hope?

PH: Yes. Can you imagine reading for pleasure, or even for sustained instruction, from a machine? Being tied to electric outlets? Hauling the contraption around in a pick-up truck? Being slave to power failures or dead batteries? Absorbing over a lifetime the accumulation of radioactive effects? Steadily damaging your eyesight by staring into the source of light instead of seeing by its reflection? Hearing the clicks and buzzes of operative energy behind the screen? You will find the countervailing advantages of the book in my essay "The Climate of Books."

Notes

Nueva Granada

Portions of this essay are reprinted from *Texas Books in Review* 5 (1983): 7–9 and the *Chicago Tribune* February 14, 1983, pp. 1, 7 by permission of the author.

Albuquerque as Recurrent Frontier in The Common Heart

This essay is reprinted from The *New Mexico Humanities Review.* (Summer, 1980): 23–33

Calliope and Clio: River Muses

A version of this essay was presented as a Carl Becker Memorial Lecture in the spring of 1982 at the University of Northern Iowa. It is reprinted from *Southwest Review* 69 (Winter, 1984): 2–15 by permission of the author.

1. Paul Horgan, *Great River* (New York: Rinehart, 1954), vii. Future references are cited parenthetically.

2. Wallace Stegner, "Born a Square," in *The Sound of Mountain Water* (New York: Doubleday, 1969), 170–85.

3. Harvey Fergusson, *Rio Grande* (New York: William Morrow, 1955); Erna Fergusson, *Our Southwest* (New York: Alfred A. Knopf, 1951); Laura Gilpin, *The Rio Grande: River of Destiny* (New York: Duell, Sloan, and Pearce, 1949); Gaspar Perez de Villagrá, *La Historia de Nuevo México* (Los Angeles: Quivira Society, 1933); Charles F. Lummis, *The Land of Poco Tiempo* (New York: Scribners, 1983).

4. Mabel Major and T. M. Pearce, *Southwest Heritage* (Albuquerque: University of New Mexico Press, 1972), 27.

5. Stanley Walker, "Long River, Long Book," *New Yorker* 30 (Dec. 4, 1954): 229.

6. D. H. Lawrence, "New Mexico," *Phoenix: The Posthumous Papers* (New York: Viking Press, 1936), 142.

7. Rudolfo Anaya, "The Writer's Landscape: Epiphany in Landscape," *Latin American Literary Review* 5 (Spring–Summer, 1977): 99.

8. See Thomas Hornsby Ferril, "Writing in the Rockies," *Rocky Mountain Reader,* ed. Ray B. West, Jr. (New York, 1946), 396; Richard West Sellers, "The Interrelationships of Literature, History and Geography in Western Writing," *Western Historical Quarterly* 4 (April, 1973): 178.

9. Sellers, 179.

10. See James West Davidson and Mark Hamilton Lytle, *After the Fact: The Art of Historical Detection* (New York: Alfred A. Knopf, 1982).

11. Davidson and Lytle, *After the Fact,* vi.

12. Barbara Tuchman, "The Historian as Artist," *Practicing History* (New York: Alfred A. Knopf, 1981), 45.

13. Tuchman, "Historian as Artist," 45.

14. Tuchman, "Historian as Artist," 46.

15. David Levin, *In Defense of Historical Literature* (New York: Hill & Wang, 1967), 1.

16. Levin, *In Defense,* 2.

17. Morroe Berger, *Real and Imagined Worlds: The Novel and Social Science* (Cambridge: Harvard University Press, 1977), 258.

18. Wallace Stegner, "On the Writing of History," in *The Sound of Mountain Water,* 205.

19. Frank D. Reeve, "A Letter to Clio," *New Mexico Historical Review* 31, 2 (1956): 132.

20. Reeve, "Letter," 131.

21. Reeve, "Letter," 131.

22. Reeve, "Letter," 131.

23. Reeve, "Letter," 130.

24. Letter, Erna Fergusson to Paul Horgan, 1954. See Catherine C. Mundell, "Paul Horgan and the Indians: *Great River* as a Historical Failure," unpublished M.A. thesis, University of Texas at El Paso, 1971.

25. See Page Smith, *The Historian and History* (New York: Alfred A. Knopf, 1964), 111–12.

26. Richard W. Etulain, "Western Fiction and History: A Reconsideration," *The American West,* ed. Jerome O. Steffen (Norman: University of Oklahoma Press, 1979), 152–74. Don D. Walker, *Clio's Cowboys* (Lincoln: University of Nebraska Press, 1981).

The Biography of Place

A version of this essay is reprinted from the *Prairie Schooner* by permission of the University of Nebraska Press. Copyright © 1981 University of Nebraska Press.

1. Paul Horgan, "The Pleasures and Perils of Regionalism," *Western American Literature* 8 (Winter 1974): 167–71. Subsequent references to this article are given as "P&P" with page numbers.

2. Forrest G. Wagner and Margaret G. Robinson, "An Interview with Wallace Stegner," *American West* 15 (Jan.-Feb., 1978): 61.

3. James M. Day, *Paul Horgan* (Austin, Tex.: Steck-Vaughn, 1967), 37, says of Horgan's regionalism: "Horgan is known primarily as a regionalist, but it should be said that he is such in the highest and best sense of the term. He is a regionalist in his settings and characters, but in his themes he is universal." See also Paul Horgan, "The Western Writer: A Symposium," *South Dakota Review* 2 (Autumn, 1964): 27–32. Asked if he is conscious of being a western writer, Horgan replies, "Since I have written about many parts of the United States, I do not comfortably wear the title 'regionalist'" (27). Among western novels he considers outstanding, Horgan lists Willa Cather first, saying about *Death Comes for the Archbishop* and others: "In all of these there is a glowing presence of the land and the light over it, against which, without undue limitation by regional reverence, the universal concerns of her characters call into play Miss Cather's quiet art. Yet she does, of course, catch most evocatively the particular homeliness of her western places, and we enjoy those for what they are" (30–31).

4. Paul Horgan, *Figures in a Landscape* (New York: Harper, 1940), 2–3.

5. Paul Horgan, "Preface to an Unwritten Book," *Yale Review* 15 (March, 1976): 324.

6. Horgan, "Preface," 325.

7. Horgan, "Preface," 325.

8. Horgan, "The Western Writer," 32.

9. Paul Horgan, "In Search of the Archbishop," *Catholic Historical Review* 46 (Jan., 1961): 413.

10. Horgan, "Archbishop," 412.

11. Horgan, "The Western Writer," 32.

12. Horgan, "Archbishop," 415, 419, 422.

13. Willa Cather, "On *Death Comes for the Archbishop*," in *On Writing* (New York: Alfred A. Knopf, 1949), 3–17. The letter was addressed to the editor of the *Commonweal*, Nov. 23, 1927.

14. Cather, "On *Death Comes*," 5.

15. Cather, "On *Death Comes*," 9.

New Mexico's Own Chronicle Revisited

A version of this essay is reprinted from *Southwestern American Literature* 5 (Fall, 1988), 5–18 by permission of the author.

1. William E. Gibbs and Alfred L. Castle, "Maurice Garland Fulton: Historian of New Mexico and the Southwest," *New Mexico Historical Review* 55, 2 (April, 1980).

2. Letter, Paul Horgan to R. F. Gish, February 18, 1987. Gibbs and Castle, "Maurice Garland Fulton," report that Fulton began work on *Chronicle* in 1934 and "shortly thereafter asked Horgan to join him" and, again, according to Horgan, that the "whole concept of the book belonged to Fulton (125)."

3. T. M. Pearce, "Los Paisanos," *New Mexico Quarterly* (May, 1936), 142.

4. Maurice Garland Fulton to Horgan, March 29, 1950, Special Collections, University of Arizona Library, Tucson.

5. Gibbs and Castle, "Maurice Garland Fulton," 125.

6. Robert F. Gish, *Paul Horgan* (Boston: Twayne Publishers, 1983), 88, observes that *Chronicle* is a significant precursor to Horgan's later, major southwestern histories just as it incorporates much of his "About the Southwest" essay, especially in the last pages entitled "The Three Southwestern Peoples." See also Eugene Taylor Jackman, *The New Mexico Military Institute 1891–1966: A Critical History*, Ph.D. dissertation, University of Mississippi, 1967, 508, where Jackman notes that "actually the central theme of the work may be detected much earlier in Horgan's thinking and writing. In an article . . . in the *Southwest Review* in 1933, the author had already spoken of a heroic triad: Indians, Spanish, and American pioneers." Jackman concludes that Horgan took the view that in New Mexico "there had been remarkably little mixing of the races" and that the "influence of Maurice G. Fulton . . . may also be seen." A more likely influence on the historical assumptions of both Horgan and Fulton is Frederick Jackson Turner and his thesis of recurrent frontiers, as well as Harvey Fergusson's *Rio Grande*. See in this regard, Robert F. Gish, "Pretty, But Is It History?: The Legacy of Harvey Fergusson's *Rio Grande*," *New Mexico Historical Review* 60, 2 (April, 1985): 173–92.

7. Gibbs and Castle, "Maurice Garland Fulton," 121.

8. Letter, Paul Horgan to Lawrence Clark Powell, March, 1971. Letter in possession of Powell. According to Gibbs and Castle, "Maurice Garland Fulton,"

Fulton's great work was to be a "history of Lincoln County in the 1870s and 1880s" (131). It is intriguing to think that if Horgan is right, what eventually became a general history of Lincoln County began as a biography of Billy the Kid. A posthumous version of Fulton's history was published by the University of Arizona Press in 1968, edited by Robert N. Mullin, and titled *Maurice G. Fulton's History of the Lincoln County War.*

9. Letter, Paul Horgan to L. C. Powell, March, 1971.

10. Letter, Paul Horgan to L. C. Powell, February 18, 1971.

11. Book jacket, Maurice Garland Fulton and Paul Horgan, eds., *New Mexico's Own Chronicle,* (Dallas: Banks Upshaw, 1937).

12. Letter, Paul Horgan to M. G. Fulton, March 29, 1950.

13. Letter, Paul Horgan to R. F. Gish, March 14, 1981.

14. See, for example, *El Paso Herald-Post,* March 20, 1937, 4.

15. *Forth Worth Morning Star–Telegram,* June 6, 1937.

16. *El Paso Times,* May 23, 1937.

17. *El Paso Times,* May 23, 1937.

18. *Houston Chronicle,* July 4, 1937.

19. *Washington Star,* May 29, 1937.

20. *Cincinnati Enquirer,* July 17, 1937.

21. *New York Times Book Review,* June 6, 1937.

22. Letter, Paul Horgan to M. G. Fulton, March, 1950.

23. Letter, Paul Horgan to R. F. Gish, March 14, 1981.

24. Gish, *Paul Horgan,* 86.

25. Howard R. Lamar, "Paul Horgan's History," *Wesleyan Library Notes* 18 (Winter, 1984): 6.

26. Lamar, "Paul Horgan's History," 7.

27. Lamar, "Paul Horgan's History," 7.

Calculating the Distance

A version of this essay is reprinted from the *Hawaii Review* 16 (Spring, 1992): 155–59 by permission of the author.

1. Paul Horgan, "Willa Cather's Incalculable Distance," in *A Certain Climate: Essays in History, Arts, and Letters* (Middletown, Conn.: Wesleyan University Press, 1988), 79–91.

2. "Paul Horgan Gets Vibes Visiting His Native Buffalo." *Buffalo Courier Express,* Oct. 4, 1977.

3. Paul Horgan, "Preface to an Unwritten Book," *Yale Review* 15 (March, 1976); Paul Horgan, "The Pleasures and Perils of Regionalism." *Western American Literature* 8, 4 (Winter, 1974): 167–71; Paul Horgan, "In Search of the Archbishop," *Catholic Historical Review* 66, 4 (Jan., 1961): 409–27.

4. See Robert F. Gish, "Willa Cather in New Mexico," *New Mexico Historical Review* 64, 2 (April, 1989): 220–29, for comment on the "tensions of geography" at work in Cather's wanderings from Virginia to Nebraska, to Pennsylvania, New York, New Hampshire, Canada, and France. As for Cather's sojourn in New Mexico, Gish observes, "It can be argued that Cather's impressions of New Mexico, beautiful and deep and sincere as they were, needed more duration, more seasoning" (228).

5. See Gish, "Willa Cather in New Mexico," where the point is made that like Lamy and Cather's fictionalized version, Latour, "Cather remained something of a tourist, a visitor" (228).

6. Willa Cather, "On *Death Comes for the Archbishop*," in *On Writing* (New York: Alfred A. Knopf, 1949), 3–17.

7. See Robert F. Gish, "Paul Horgan and the Biography of Place," *Prairie Schooner,* 55, 1–2 (Spring–Summer, 1981): 226–32.

Legacy: The Great Literatus

A version of this essay was first presented as a speech at the DeGolyer Library, Southern Methodist University, Sept. 21, 1991.

1. Walt Whitman, "A National Literature," in *The Harper American Literature,* ed. Donald McQuade et al. (New York: Harper and Row, 1987), 168.

2. Whitman, "A National Literature," 163.

3. Ralph Waldo Emerson, "The American Scholar," *Ralph Waldo Emerson* (New York: Oxford University Press, 1990), 37.

4. See "The Enduring Values of Paul Horgan: Reviews and Interview by Robert F. Gish," *Bloomsbury Review* (Jan.–Feb., 1989), 8.

5. "Enduring Values," 10.

6. "Enduring Values," 10. See also Robert F. Gish, "'Pretty, But Is It History,' The Legacy of Harvey Fergusson's *Rio Grande*," *New Mexico Historical Review,* 60, 2 (1985): 173–92.

The Centuries of Santa Fe: A New Perspective

This essay was written as an afterword for the 1993 reissue of *Centuries* by the University of New Mexico Press.

Completive Polarities: Interview

This interview was recorded at Paul Horgan's home in Middletown, Connecticut, in June of 1979 and the transcripts are published here for the first time.

The Enduring Values of Paul Horgan: Interview

This interview is reprinted from the *Bloomsbury Review*, 9 (Jan.–Feb., 1989): 8–10 by permission of Robert F. Gish.

Bibliography

Works by Paul Horgan

Note: The major collections of Horgan's writings are at the Beinecke Library, Yale University; Southern Methodist University, DeGolyer Library; New Mexico Military Institute Library; and the University of New Mexico Library.

Approaches to Writing. New York: Farrar, Straus & Giroux, 1973. Nonfiction. "Bibliography, The." In *Approaches to Writing,* ed. James Kraft. 237–332. Primary.

Centuries of Santa Fe, The. New York: Dutton, 1956. Historical sketches.

Certain Climate, A: Essays in History, Arts, and Letters. Middletown, Conn.: Wesleyan University Press, 1988. Essays.

Citizen of New Salem. New York: Farrar, Straus & Cudahy, 1961. Biography.

Clerihews of Paul Horgan, The. Middletown, Conn.: Wesleyan University Press, 1985.

Common Heart, The. New York: Harper, 1942. Novel.

Conquistadors in North American History. New York: Farrar, Straus, 1963

Conquistadors in North America. London: Macmillan, 1963. History.

"Critical Preface." *Selected Poems of Witter Bynner* (New York: Alfred A. Knopf, 1936), xxiii–lxix.

Devil in the Desert, The. New York: Longmans, Green, 1952. Novella.

Distant Trumpet, A. New York: Farrar, Straus & Cudahy, 1960. Novel.

Encounters with Stravinsky. New York: Farrar, Straus & Giroux, 1972. Memoir.

Everything to Live For. New York: Farrar, Straus & Giroux, 1968. Novel.

Far from Cibola. New York: Harper, 1938. Novel.

Fault of Angels, The. New York: Harper, 1936. Novel.

Figures in a Landscape. New York: Harper, 1940. Stories and essays.

Foreword. *N. C. Wyeth* by Douglas Allen & Douglas Allen, Jr. (New York: Crown, 1972), 11–13.

"Foreword." *Santa Fe* by Oliver La Farge (Norman: University of Oklahoma Press, 1959), v–x.

From the Royal City of the Holy Faith of St. Francis of Assisi. Santa Fe: Rydal, 1936. Historical sketches.

Give Me Possession. New York: Farrar, Straus & Cudahy, 1957. Novel.

Great River: The Rio Grande in North American History. New York: Rinehart, 1954. History.

Habit of Empire, The. Santa Fe: Rydal, 1939. Novel.

Henriette Wyeth. Chadds Ford, Penn.: Brandywine River Museum, 1980. Biography.

Heroic Triad, The: Essays in the Social Energies of Three Southwestern Cultures. New York: Holt, Rinehart & Winston, 1970.

Humble Powers. London: Macmillan, 1954; New York: Image, 1955. Stories.

Josiah Gregg and His Vision of the Early West. New York: Farrar, Straus & Giroux, 1979. Biography.

Lamp on the Plains, A. New York: Harper, 1937. Novel.

Lamy of Santa Fe: His Life and Times. New York: Farrar, Straus & Giroux, 1975. Biography.

Main Line West. New York: Harper, 1936. Novel.

Maurice Baring Restored: Selections from His Work. Ed. with intro. and commentaries. New York: Farrar, Straus & Giroux, 1970.

Memories of the Future. New York: Farrar, Straus & Giroux, 1966. Novel.

Men of Arms. Philadelphia: McKay, 1931. Children's nonfiction.

Mexico Bay: A Novel of the Mid-Century. New York: Farrar, Straus & Giroux, 1982. Novel.

Mountain Standard Time: Main Line West, Far from Cibola, The Common Heart. New York: Farrar, Straus & Cudahy, 1962.

New Mexico's Own Chronicle: Three Races in the Writings of Four Hundred Years, ed. with Maurice Garland Fulton. Dallas: Banks Upshaw, 1937. Historical anthology.

No Quarter Given. New York: Harper, 1935. Novel.

Of America East and West, intro. by Henry Steele Commager. New York: Farrar, Straus & Giroux, 1984.

One of the Quietest Things. Los Angeles: University of California School of Library Service, 1960. Speech.

One Red Rose for Christmas. New York: Longmans, Green, 1952. Novella.

Peach Stone, The: Stories from Four Decades. New York: Farrar, Straus & Giroux, 1967.

Peter Hurd: A Portrait Sketch from Life. Austin: University of Texas Press, 1965. Biography.

Return of the Weed, The. New York: Harper, 1936; *Lingering Walls.* London: Constable, 1936. Stories.

Rome Eternal. New York: Farrar, Straus & Cudahy, 1959. Television narration.

Saintmaker's Christmas Eve, The. New York: Farrar, Straus & Cudahy, 1955. Novella.

Songs after Lincoln. New York: Farrar, Straus & Giroux, 1965. Poetry.

Thin Mountain Air, The. New York: Farrar, Straus & Giroux, 1977. Novel.

Things as They Are. New York: Farrar, Straus, 1964. Novel.

Toby and the Nighttime. New York: Farrar, Straus, 1963. Children's story.

Under the Sangre de Cristo. Santa Fe: Rydal, 1985; Flagstaff: Northland, 1985. Historical sketches.

Whitewater. New York: Farrar, Straus & Giroux, 1970. Novel.

Writer's Eye, A. New York: Abrams, 1988. Notes and watercolors.

Critical Studies of Horgan

Carter, Alfred. "On the Fiction of Paul Horgan." *New Mexico Quarterly* 7 (Aug., 1937), 207–16.

Day, James M. *Paul Horgan.* Austin, Tex.: Steck-Vaughn, 1967.

Gish, Robert F. "Albuquerque as Recurrent Frontier in *The Common Heart.*" *New Mexico Historical Review* 3 (Summer, 1980), 23–33.

———. "Calliope and Clio: Paul Horgan's River Muses." *Southwest Review* 69 (Winter, 1984), 2–15.

———. "*New Mexico's Own Chronicle* Revisited." *Southwestern American Literature,* 14 (Fall, 1988), 5–18.

————. *Paul Horgan.* Boston: Twayne, 1983.

————. "Paul Horgan." *A Literary History of the American West* (Fort Worth: Texas Christian University Press, 1987), 574–86.

————. "Paul Horgan and the Biography of Place." *Prairie Schooner* 55 (Spring–Summer, 1981), 226–32.

Kraft, James. "About *Things As They Are.*" *Canadian Review of American Studies* 2 (Spring, 1971), 48–52.

————. "No Quarter Given: An Essay on Paul Horgan." *Southwest Historical Quarterly* 80 (July, 1976), 1–32.

McCullough, David. "Historian, and Much, Much More." *New York Times Book Review* (8 April, 1984), 3, 22.

Pilkington, William T. "Paul Horgan." *My Blood's Country: Studies in Southwestern Literature* (Fort Worth: Texas Christian University Press, 1973), 51–64.

Symposium. *South Dakota Review* 2 (Autumn, 1964), 27–32.

Index

Acoma, ix, 38, 75, 78
Addison, Joseph, 34
Adventures of Huckleberry Finn, 29
Albuquerque, N. Mex., ix, xi, 3, 5, 15–24, 41–42, 61–62, 78, 87, 89–90, 93
Albuquerque High School, 41
Albuquerque Journal, 93
Amarillo, Tex., 4
Anaya, Rudolfo, 32
Apache-Cavalry wars, 26
Apache Indians, 78
Aragon, Ray John de, 78
Arizona, 4
Arizona Highways, 92
Army Information Branch, 96
Aspects of the Novel, 98
Austin, Tex., 59
Auvergne, France, 43
Aztlán, 37, 68

ballet: Russian, 84
Bandelier, Adolph, 77
Banks Upshaw (publishers), 47, 51–52
Baptist: Southern, ix
Baring, Maurice, 104
Becker, Carl, 35, 38
Beinecke Library, 85
Berger, Morroe, 35
Billy the Kid, 47, 50–51, 53, 125

biography: as art, 70, 99–100, 112–14
Birmingham News, 53
Bloomsbury Review, xiv
Boca Chica, 9
Booth, Wayne, 60
Bradley, Jerry, xiii
Brand, Max, 29
Bronco, 49
Brownsville, Tex., 9
Buffalo, N. Y., 41, 75, 90–91
Burke, Edmund, 34
Bush, President George, 115
Bynner Foundation, 83
Bynner, Witter, 5, 81, 83, 103, 117

California, 4, 19
Calliope, 27
Canada, 4
Capra, Frank, 97, 103
Carlyle, Thomas, 112
Carson, Kit, 77
Castle, Alfred, 46, 48, 50–51
Castor, 25
Cather, Elsie, 41, 64
Cather, Willa, 39–44, 58–66, 81, 90, 99, 116, 123; and impresions of New Mexico, 126; and "tensions of geography," 126. Works: *Death Comes for the Archbishop*, 6, 40, 44,

64, 116, 123; "A Death in the
Desert," 64; "Letter to
Commonweal," 44; "The Sculptor's
Funeral," 64; "A Wagner Matinee,"
61, 64
Catholic Historical Review, 59
Catholicism, ix, 15, 27, 44, 79, 94–95
Cavett, Dick, 84
Chadds Ford, Del., 90
Chicano: as cultural identity, 91
Churchill, Winston, 35
Cibola, 37
Cincinnati, Ohio, 43
Cincinnati Enquirer, 54
Cisneros, Jose, 4
City of Faith, 62, 79. *See also* Santa Fe
Civil War, 53
Clerihews, 117
Clermont-Ferrand, France, 43
Clio, 27
Commanger, Henry Steele, 82
Commerce on the Prairies (Gregg): 47, 51
Coronado, Juan Vasques de, 56
Corpus Christi, Tex., 4
Craft, Robert, 83–84
Crime and Punishment, x

Dallas, Tex., 47
Dancing Gods (Fergusson): 48
Davidson, James West, 33–34
DeGolyer, Library, 5, 129
Delacroix, Eugene, 28
Diary and Letters of Josiah Gregg, The,
49. *See also* Fulton, Maurice
Garland
Dickens, Charles, 35
Dobie, J. Frank, 4, 64, 83
Dukakis, Governor Michael, 115
Durango, Mex., 43

Eastman School of Music, 50
Eliot, T. S., 107

El Paso, Tex., 31
El Paso Library Association, 4
El Paso Times, 53
Emerson, Ralph Waldo, 68
Engle, Paul, 86. *See also* University of
Iowa
e pluribus unum, 76, 90–91
ethnobiography, 25
ethnohistory, 25, 33
Etulain, Richard W., 38

Facts on File, xiv
Farmer, David, xiii
Farrar Straus (publishers), 102, 105, 107
Faulkner, William, 35
Fearns, Reverend John M., 43
feminism, 10, 69, 104–105
Fergusson, Erna, 30, 37, 48, 90, 93
Fergusson, Harvey, 30, 48, 83, 90–91.
See also Frontier's End
Ferril, Thomas Hornsby, 33
Flaubert, Gustave, 104
Folklore Record, 47
Forster, E. M., 98
Fort Worth Morning Star–Telegram, 53
France, 40. *See also individual towns
and regions*
Freud, Sigmund, 99
Freudianism, 106
Frijoles Canyon, 55
frontier, 12–24, 33–34, 49
*Frontier's End: The Life and literature
of Harvey Fergusson*, 71
Fulton, Maurice Garland, 26, 45–57

Gardner, John, 106
Garrett, Pat, 50
Germany, 37
Gibbon, Edward, 35
Gibbs, William E., 46, 48, 50–51
Gibson, Walker, 60
Gilpin, Laura, 30

Giroux, Robert, 85, 107
Goodman, Ellen, 114
Gray, Thomas, 34
Greene, Graham, 95
Gregg, Josiah, 47, 48, 57, 77
Gulf of Mexico, 9, 11

Harcourt Brace (publishers), 107
Hardy, Thomas, 86
Harper (publishers), 107
Harris, Jim, xiii
Hawaii Review, xiv
Hemingway, Ernest, 29
Henderson, Charles Arthur, 26, 36
Herodotus, 28
Hertzog, Carl, 4
Hillerman, Tony, 30
historiography, 27, 38, 70, 76, 100,
 112–14
Hogan, Ray, 29
Hollywood, 97, 103
homosexuality, 10
Horgan, Paul: biography of, 28, 61,
 90; Catholicism and, 95–96; and
 class attitudes, 75; as dean of
 Southwestern writers, 4; and
 "ecology of the drawing room," 71;
 and service in World War II, 26,
 30, 96–98; as transcontinental
 writer, 87; and unity in life, 109
—, awards of: Bancroft Prize, 5, 26,
 30; Carr P. Collins Award, 5;
 Harper Prize, 3, 63; Jesse H.
 Jones Award, 5; Pulitzer Prize,
 5, 26, 30, 57, 59, 69, 73–74;
 Western Literature Association
 Distinguished Achievement
 Award, 5, 39, 59;
—, works of: "About the
 Southwest: A Panorama of
 Nueva Granada," 4–5, 26, 48;
 "Allegory," 119; *Approaches to*

Writing, 82, 85, 106; *Centuries of
 Santa Fe*, 26, 41, 49, 73–79, 87,
 92; *A Certain Climate*, 58–66,
 111, 119; *The Clerihews of Paul
 Horgan*, 49, 117; *The Common
 Heart*, 12–24, 56, 87, 92; "The
 Climate of Books," 111, 119;
*Conquistadors in North American
 History*, xi, 26, 49, 115; "The
 Devil In the Desert, 6; *A
 Distant Trumpet*, xi, 26, 87, 96;
Everything to Live For, 90; *Far
 From Cibola*, xi, 3, 87, 102; *The
 Fault of Angels*, 3, 50, 63; *Figures
 In A Landscape*, 41; *From The
 Royal City*, 26, 50; *Give Me
 Possession*, 87; *The Golden Rose*,
 106; *Great River*, 5–6, 11, 25–38,
 40, 49, 55, 73–75, 94, 105, 107–
 108, 115; *The Habit of Empire*, 26,
 30, 38, 49, 75; "The Head of the
 House of Wattleman," 63;
Henriette Wyeth, 49; *The Heroic
 Triad*, xi, 26, 40, 49; "In Search
 of the Archbishop," 59; "In
 Summer's Name," 6; *Josiah
 Gregg and His Vision of the
 Early West*, xi, 26, 50; *A Lamp
 On The Plains*, 6, 50; *Lamy of
 Santa Fe*, xi, 26, 40–42, 49, 73,
 115; *Main Line West*, 6, 50;
Memories of the Future, 87, 100,
 107; *Men At Arms*, 105; *Mexico
 Bay*, xi, 3–4, 7–9, 26, 56;
Mountain Standard Time, xi;
New Mexico's Own Chronicle, 26,
 45–57; *No Quarter Given*, xi, 13,
 50, 102, 108; "Old Army," 97;
 "The Pleasures and Perils of
 Regionalism," 39, 59, 65;
 "Preface to an Unwritten
 Book," 59, 65; "Rain In

Laredo," 7–8; *The Reach Stone*, xi, 6, 7, 59, 81, 97; *Return of the Weed*, 50; *The Richard Trilogy*, 3, 75, 90, 101; *Rome Eternal*, 94; "So Little Freedom," 6, 81, 117; *The Thin Mountain Air*, 3, 13, 75, 87–88, 91, 104; *Toby and the Nighttime*, 105; "Toward A Redefinition of Progress," 5; *A Tree on the Plains*, 6; *Under the Sangre de Cristo*, 111, 117, 131; *Whitewater*, 5–7, 10, 80, 87, 96; "Willa Cather's Incalculable Distance," 58–66; *The Writer's Eye*, 111, 115

Houston Chronicle, 53

Howlett, William Joseph, 44

Huning, Franz, 78

Hurd, Peter, 4, 90, 116; South Plains Mural, 5

Indians, 21, 31, 91. *See also individual tribes*

In the American Grain, 79

Iowa, x. *See also* University of Iowa

Isleta, 78

James, Stuart B., 34

Jamestown, 79

Journey With Genius, 81

Kearny, Stephen Watts, 18–20, 57, 77

Keats, John, 24

Knopf, Alfred A., 111

La Farge, Oliver, 5, 37, 74, 92, 94

La Fonda Hotel, 42, 62–63, 66, 116

La Historia de Nuevo Mexico, 30

Lamar, Howard, 56

L'Amour, Louis, 29

Lamy, Jean Baptiste, 40–43, 57–66, 77–78, 99, 116–17

"landscape mysticism," 33

Lavender, David, 34

Lawrence, D. H., 30, 32, 81, 117

Lawrence, Frieda, 81, 117

Lea, Tom, 4

Leda, 25

Lempedes, France, 43

Levin, David, 35

library science, 26

Lincoln County, N. Mex., 125

Lincoln County Museum, 51

"Little Texas," 5, 6, 88

Long, Haniel, 5

Longworth, Alice Roosevelt, 116

Los Alamos, N. Mex., 37, 55

Luhan, Mabel Dodge, 31, 89, 117

Luhan, Tony, 117

Lyons, Bonnie, xiii

Lytle, Mark Hamilton, 33–34

Macaulay, Thomas B., 28

Machebeuf, Reverend Joseph, 44, 58

Macmillan (publishers), 47, 51

Magdalena, N. Mex., 87, 88

Major, Mabel, 30

Mamoulian, Rouben, 116

Manhattan Project, 54

Manzano Mountains, x

Marxism, 99, 106

Maugham, W. Somerset, 3, 11

McCarthy, Mary, 93–94

McGinnis, John, 5, 64, 82

Melville, Herman, 94

Mencken, H. L., 114,

Menninger, Gen. Will, 96

Mexican War, 7–10

Mexico, 7, 40, 43. *See also individual cities*

Middletown, Conn., 75, 89, 118

Milagro Beanfield War, The, 92

Milwaukee Journal, 53

Meining, D. W., 34
Merton, Father Thomas, 107
Mnemosyne, 25
Mundell, Catherine C., 30
Munson, E. L., 98

Napoleon, x
Narvaez, Perfilio de, 56
Nash, Roderick, 34
Native Americans, 91. *See also
   individual tribes;* Indians
nature, 119
Navajo Indians, 35, 78
Nebraska, 40, 42, 59–61
Nevins, Allen, 28
New England, 118
New Ethnicity, 68
New History, 68
New Journalism, 68
New Mexico, 118; mystique of, 54.
   See also individual places, regions
New Mexico Historical Review, 46–47
New Mexico Humanities Review, xiv
New Mexico Military Institute, 30, 46,
   49, 61, 97
New Mexico Quarterly, 47
New York (state), 3, 28, 61, 118. *See also
   individual cities*
New Yorker, 31
New York theater, 102
New York Times, 54, 74
Nichols, John, 92
novel theory, 106

O'Conner, Flannery, 87
Old Glory: An American Voyage, 29
Old Town, 18, 78. *See also*
   Albuquerque
Onate, Juan de, x, 15–16, 38, 56, 77
On Moral Fiction, 106
Oregon Trail, The, 56
Ortiz, Alfonso, 78

Pajarito, Plateau, 55
Parkman, Francis, 35, 56–57, 75
Parsons, Noel, xiii
Paul Horgan, 80
Pearce, T. M. (Matthew), 30, 47
Pecos Valley, 5, 87
Perkins, Maxwell, 107
Pierpont Morgan Library, 85
Pilkington, Tom, xiii
Pineda, Alonzo Alvarez de, 56
Pittsburgh, Pa., 61
Pollux, 25
Popé: and pueblo revolt, 78
Port Isabel, 7
Powell, Lawrence Clark, 4, 49
Prairie Schooner, xiv
presidential campaign, 1988, 115
Procrustes, 36
Proust, Marcel, 89
Pueblo Indians, 78
Puye Cliff Dwellings, 55
Pyle, Ernie, ix

Raban, Jonathan, 29
Recuerdos del Porvenir, 100
Reeve, Frank D., 29, 35–37, 74
regionalism, 86–87, 113–14, 123
"relativity of otherness," 76
religion: and art, 43. *See also individual
   faiths, denominations*
Rice, Virginia, 106–107
Rinehart (publishers), 107
Rio Bravo del Norte, 37
Rio Grande, 48
Rio Grande River, 25–26, 32, 87, 90, 119
rivers: American, 29
Rochester, N.Y., 89
Rome, 40, 79
Roswell, N. Mex., 4–5, 61, 64, 82–83,
   87–88
Roswell Museum, 51
Royal City, 79. *See also* Santa Fe

St. Francis Cathedral, 62
St. Michael's College, 62
St. Vincent's Hospital, 62
Sanchez, Archbishop Robert, 77
Sandia Mountains, x
San Diego Union, 53
Sando, Joe, 78
San Felipe de Neri Church, 19
San Patricio, 87, 89
Santa Clara Pueblo, 55
Santa Fe, N. Mex., 5, 32, 39–40, 42–43,
   48, 53, 62, 74, 77, 79, 82–83, 89, 102,
   117
Santa Fe New Mexican, 94
Santo Domingo, 78
Saturday Evening Post, 7
Saxton, Eugene, 107
Sellers, Richard West, 33
sexuality: in fiction, 104
Shelley, Percy Bysshe, 24
Shepard, Paul, 34
Simmons, Marc, 34
Smith, Henry Nash, 34
Snow, C. P., 83
Socorro, 88
Southern Methodist University, 5, 69,
   82
Southwest Renaissance, 64, 69, 82–83
Southwest Review, xiv, 5, 26, 48–49
"spot of time," 88
Stafford, Jean, 107
Stallion Gate, 55
Stegner, Wallace, 29, 35, 39, 74, 91
Sterile Cuckoo, The, 92
Stevenson, Philip, 48
Straus, Roger, 107
Stravinsky, Leopold, 84
Stravinsky, Madame, 84
*Stravinsky: The Chronicle of a
   Friendship*, 83–84
style: in fiction, 71, 105
Sullivan, Maud Durlin, 4

Taos, N. Mex., 5, 39, 82, 87, 89, 92, 117
Taos Pueblo, 78
technology, 116
Texas: Panhandle, 4, 88. *See also
   individual cities*
Texas–Santa Fe Expedition, 52
Texas Tech University, 5
Thomas, Dylan, 31
Thucydides, 36
Tinkle, Lon, 82
Tolstoy, Leo, 86, 104
transcendental writers, 87
Trevelyan, George, 35
Trinity Site, 37, 55
Trojan War, x
tuberculosis, 90
Tuchman, Barbara, 34
Tulsa World, 53
Turner, Frederick, III, 34
Turner, Frederick Jackson, 33–34, 37,
   48–49, 56–57, 69, 75
Twain, Mark (Samuel Clemens), 29

University of Iowa, 86; Writers
   Workshop, 86
University of New Mexico, 47
University of New Mexico Press, 52
University of Notre Dame, 59
University of Texas, 5, 83

Vaca, Alvar Nunez Cabeza de, 56
Vargas, Don Diego de, 56, 77
Vassar, 93
Villagra, Gaspar Perez, 30
violence: in fiction, 104
Virginia (state), 42
virtual reality, 76

Walker, Don D., 38
Walker, Stanley, 31–35, 74
Walpole, Horace, 34
Washington, D.C., 4, 96

Washington Post, 4
Washington Star, 53
Webb, Walter Prescott, 64, 74, 83
Weber, David, xiii
Wellesley, 106
Wesleyan University, 61
Western Attorney, The, 18, 20–21
Whitman, Walt, 67–68, 70
Wile, Lulu, 106
Williams, William Carlos, 79
Wilmington, Del., 90
Wordsworth, William, 88
Works Program Administration
   (WPA), 51

World War II, ix, 26, 61
Wyeth, Henriette, 90, 116

Yale Review, 59
Yank, 96
Yardley, Jonathan, 4

Zaldivar, Don Vicente, 75
Zeus, 25
Zimmerman telegram, 37
Zuni, 78